I Can See Angels

I Can See Angels

by
Dawn Rawlings

*Printed in our spiritual land of Australia
and dedicated to all caretakers of this
majestic country and to all caretakers
of countries everywhere.*

— ❖ —

*Dawn Rawlings a 'proud Australian'
was born at "High Ridge"
Mount Boyce in the Blue Mountains
of New South Wales Australia.*

— ❖ —

Except for those who have given permission to appear in this book, names and identifying characteristics of individuals have been changed to protect their privacy.

DEDICATION

This book is dedicated
to
Joseph McClenton
American Humanitarian and
channel for the entity Joshua.

To the memory of
my brother
Maxwell Boyce Pemberton
in this lifetime
and to the "memory" of
other lifetimes shared with him.

A special thank you
to my Agent and friend
Mr Stephen Moriarty.

A special thank you
to my husband
Paul F. Rawlings
and to my daughter
Suellen for their support
and encouragement
in the writing
of this book.

I would also like to thank the Angels
for sending me Anna Scott,
my fabulous editor;
Shanna Provost for proofing
the first draft, and of course
the Nacson clan for
doing what they do best.

I Can See Angels

A True Adventure

**By
DAWN RAWLINGS**

© Dawn Rawlings 1995

IMPORTANT NOTICE TO READERS

The suggestions in this book for personal growth are not meant to substitute for the advice of a trained professional such as a medical doctor or psychiatrist. It is essential to consult such a professional in the case of any physical or mental symptoms. The publishers and author expressly disclaim any liability for injuries or loss resulting from use of the methods contained herein by readers.

Copyright © Dawn Rawlings
First published in 1995 By
Nacson and Sons Pty Ltd
P.O. Box 515, Brighton-Le-Sands NSW 2216
Ph: (02) 281 6179 • Fax: (02) 281 2075

ISBN: 0-947266-11-9

All rights reserved. No part of the publication may be reproduced, stored in a retrieval system, or transmitted in any form or by any means, electronic, mechanical, photocopying, recording or otherwise, without the prior permission of the copyright owner.

Printed and bound in Australia by: **McPherson's Printing Group**
Cover Design by: **Eli Nacson**
Cover Art by: **The Grail - Pamela Matthews**
Editing by: **Anna H. Scott**
Typesetting: **Rhett Nacson**

CONTENTS

Preface . . . . *Page* XI

The Dolphin Connection . . . . *Page* 1

Visions Past and Present . . . . *Page* 13

Messages from Beyond . . . . *Page* 31

Beliefs . . . . *Page* 43

Adventures of a Meditator . . . . *Page* 69

Channel-board Adventures . . . . *Page* 81

Past Lives I . . . . *Page* 103

Past Lives II . . . . *Page* 143

Confirmations . . . . *Page* 171

Leave Body - Will Travel . . . . *Page* 213

Transition . . . . *Page* 225

I Can See Angels . . . . *Page* 241

*During out-of-body experiences
I still find myself viewing my life
- present, past or future -
as an observer.
For this reason I have written the preface
in the third person.
– D.R.*

PREFACE

The child knew she'd been rushed to hospital again. She was aware of the adults' alarm as she drifted in and out of conscious life.

She liked the drifting. Liked leaving her body behind and silently drifting up, up, up - until the earth disappeared far below...

...drifting through time and space, encased in love, in bliss...

...eagerly watching now for the tiny, familiar balls of light to appear in the distance. Watching as they moved towards her like small Christmas lights, twinkling and glowing, welcoming, and radiating love.

They had greeted her many times before. She loved her meetings with them.

And she loved the way they grew little wings as they approached, transforming until they appeared as tiny golden Angels.

"Funny!" she thought, "There's no Heaven or Hell here! And Isn't God supposed to notice if I'm good or bad? Why do grown-ups tell such stories? They're so silly. When I grow up I won't tell children untrue stories."

From the earth far below, a doctor's voice boomed out. "She's going! She's dying! Be quick or we'll lose her!"

"Rubbish!" the child thought, "I'm not dying, I'm not going - I am only looking. In fact, I'm only visiting. That's all I'm doing, I am visiting."

As she spoke, the child knew she had returned to her body. "I won't visit anymore, I won't. Because every time I have fun drifting off to meet my Angels, the hospital people push tubes up my nose."

She felt the tube forcing down her throat. The pain made her cry. It was just like punishment - pain followed by tears.

PREFACE

At the tender age of five the child made up her mind.

"I'll get better. I'll be a good girl, I'll stop talking to Angels. I'm going home and I won't come back here anymore."

And she never did.

This was not an earth-shattering experience.

But it did create a ripple of strength. The five-year-old quietly knew that somehow, deep down, she alone was in control of her living and dying.

She also knew that when she finally did die, it would be fun and something to look forward to.

After her return from hospital, her knight in shining armor - her brother Roy - taught her to walk again. Every day after school, he helped her. First to hold onto the kitchen table, and then to stagger around and around it.

He patiently worked with her until she could walk alone.

Only once did a lapse occur. The little balls of light appeared and she started to talk to them. "Are you talking to Angels again?" Roy asked.

"No," she said, not wishing to alarm him, "I'm only counting them."

At her check-up the doctor said, "Her kidneys are irreparably damaged. She will always have trouble with them."

"Oh, no I won't!" she thought strongly.

And she never did!

As a child she learned about choice. "If I say something I shouldn't say, or do something I shouldn't do, I know I will be punished."

Sometimes she made the right choice. And many times she didn't.

But her actions always caused a reaction. If she was a "good" girl, her mother approved of her. If, however, she was a "bad" girl, she made Mother angry.

She often marveled at the power she possessed. Sometimes her power frightened her. Was it possible that she alone controlled her destiny? Was it possible that her very own choices in life, at every turn, decided the outcome of everything that happened? This was "heavy stuff". Too heavy for a child to handle.

The child decided to conform, and almost gave her power away. She went to church and learned the Bible from start to finish, hating the parts about God demanding animal sacrifices. From her near-death experiences she knew the God Force did not judge, and certainly wouldn't demand the sacrifice of animals.

She knew all that existed out there was pure love; and that God/Goddess was, in fact, pure love. Her favorite saying became, "Jesus never wrote any part of this Bible". And reveled in the stony silences that followed.

She tried to conform.

She really tried.

But she never quite allowed her wings to be clipped.

Communications now were with Goddesses, Fairies, Extraterrestrials and Devas. Teachers thought she had a "wonderful imagination".

The family reacted angrily if she discussed the talks she'd had with Uncle Harry, however. He'd died long before she was born. They said that only very evil and wicked people talked to the dead.

This made the child sad. She yearned to be approved of - but talking to Uncle Harry was fun.

Decisions! decisions! "If I choose to tell them, I'll be in big trouble. If I choose not to tell them, they won't be angry at all."

If she alone made the choice then, of course, she was the one with the power. Adults could yell and smack as much as they liked. They were like puppets. They always reacted to the choices she made.

She alone created the outcome!

Many years later, both Seth (who channeled through Jane Roberts before her death in 1985) and Lazaris (who has never lived on the Earth and who channels through Jach Purcel) confirmed everything the child already knew.

CHAPTER ONE

The Dolphin Connection

Past lives in place of future Predictions ... *Page* 3

The Lazaris Dolphin Calendar .... *Page* 9

PAST LIVES IN PLACE OF
FUTURE PREDICTIONS

It was late on a Saturday afternoon and my last client was an old friend.

Raymondo was looking forward to a session on his future. He and Maggie had been married for almost six months and I knew he had many questions to ask.

Suddenly I felt a familiar tap on the back of my head - the sign I receive when a message is "coming through" to me.

I found myself saying, "Raymondo, I am not going to read for you today. Instead, I'll put you back to past lives and see if you've shared any lives with Maggie."

"Why did I say that?" I thought.

Past lives instead of future predictions?

I don't know where this tapping comes from or why I receive it. The sensation is similar to when someone taps you on the shoulder to get your attention.

The only difference is that the taps are on the back of my head and, at the same time, names or messages are "with me".

If I hold back from giving out the message, the tapping becomes stronger.

On a few occasions, I've been tapped on the forehead as I was about to say something, and have immediately held back.

The tap on the forehead seems to be a "no" signal.

Sometimes one tap comes, sometimes two or three. Then the words seem to flow from within.

They tumble out. I become aware of the content only after I've said it.

"Why not?" said Raymondo. "Past lives it is."

I applied hypnosis and suggested that he may like to remember all details of the session. I also suggested he speak loudly and clearly, and in English.

Raymondo's breathing became slower and slower. He moaned softly. He was now in trance.

"I have found a life with Maggie. We're swimming together. There is no end to the water, it seems to stretch forever - there is nothing else but water."

"Are you sure?" I asked. "Surely you are near land or a boat?"

"No! no! We are dolphins, beautiful dolphins. Maggie and I are both dolphins.

"We are with our friends, swimming underwater and leaping over the waves whenever we surface, then swimming as fast as we can. I have trouble keeping up with her."

"Is this a happy life?" I asked.

"Oh yes! Very happy...until we become separated."

Tears streamed down his cheeks.

"I can't find her. I'm searching and searching. I just cannot locate her."

"Let's go forward in this life you're experiencing; go forward until you find her, Raymondo. Keep going, keep going now, further and further until you find her."

"I never find her, I never do," he sobbed, "I spend my whole life searching, in vain."

Immediately I suggested we move on from the dolphin lifetime and find out if another life existed with Maggie, preferably a happy life.

We found such a lifetime, in a different time and space.

A life on another planet, a very dry and desolate place.

They were both young men, serving together on a mission. At this point in time they were waiting patiently to "be picked up by a passing airship" *(quote).*

The session ended and we moved to the kitchen for coffee and a chat.

We were both intrigued by their Animal Kingdom life together as dolphins.

"I'm so pleased I experienced past lives today," Raymondo said. "But why did you alter my session from a future Reading to past lives? Was there a special reason?"

"I honestly can't explain it," I replied, "I was as surprised as you were when I suggested it.

"It almost seems as if a past-life experience was of more importance to you today than a Reading on your future would be. I'm just as baffled as you are."

Raymondo and Maggie went to dinner at a favorite restaurant that evening. The main topic of conversation centered around their previous lifetimes together.

Before they met in this life, they had both taken on the Buddhist faith. Raymondo had a strict Catholic upbringing, Maggie's family were born-again Christians, and yet they both chose to be Buddhists.

Now, over a romantic dinner, they renewed their wedding vows to each other.

The next morning Maggie rose early and jogged alone along the beach she loved so much. It was something she liked to do most Sundays.

She never returned.

Maggie was killed that day.

Maggie's name is written on my bright-pink channel board, along with the names of my brother and other friends who have "passed over".

I use the channel board as a means to converse with them, to keep in touch, happily and safely.

My personal channel "board" is best explained as looking not unlike a place mat, with letters of the alphabet, numerals and a few words written on it. It is a successful way of communicating with "the other side".

Maggie and I communicate often.

Her experiences in this life, and in other lives she shared with her killer, could fill more than one book.

THE LAZARIS DOLPHIN CALENDAR

After the funeral, Raymondo went away for a few days, courtesy of the airline they'd both traveled with extensively for their work.

The destination turned out to be Sea World on the Gold Coast in Queensland.

From his hotel window, he watched the dolphins swim in their pool. Outside his door were two golden statues of dolphins.

When he returned, Raymondo and I "talked" to Maggie on my channel board.

To do this we place a small crystal, or a coin, on the Star at the top of the board, and ask for only a High Level Consciousness to come through with love.

I have an extremely loving and helpful guide called "John". John was successful in bringing Maggie through, thus allowing Romando to have an in-depth conversation with her.

When we were about to finish, John spelled out the words - "Dawn, Lazaris wants to speak to you."

I was amazed!

Lazaris wanting to talk to me!

Sure, I had conversed with him quite often on the channel board, but I'd always asked for him to come through. This time he was asking for me.

Lazaris spelt out his message to me.

"Dawn, may we suggest you give Raymondo your spare Lazaris dolphin calendar - With love."

And was gone!

Lazaris is a non-physical entity, a consciousness

without form, who channels through an American, Jach Purcel.

Lazaris is extraordinary, unique. Many people say, "There is channeling, and then there is Lazaris". The workshops and sessions with this loving entity are taped and distributed worldwide. I receive all the tapes and work with them constantly.

He is "wise beyond what we have known, loving beyond what we have conceived, and committed to each of us in our search for enlightenment. He is a delightful friend - a gentle and powerful guide for our journey home to God/Goddess/All that is." **

Lazaris communicates with us by "channeling", which is perhaps best described by Lazaris:

"In order to communicate with you, we send forth a series of vibrations. These vibratory frequencies go through a series of 'step-down generations' until they can safely enter your reality.

"The energy field of the one you call Jach acts like an antenna; his body, like an amplifier. ... When we communicate we are not in the body - how archaic! Such behavior is no more necessary than having your nightly newscaster actually be in your television set! ... The best way to keep the information pure is to have the channel be as much a 'pure instrument' as possible." **

Only Lazaris could have known I had a spare Lazaris dolphin calendar. My dear friend had come through with a loving suggestion, to help Raymondo in his time of grief.

**(Quotes taken from LAZARIS INTERVIEWS BOOK 1 Concept: Synergy Publishing.)

CHAPTER TWO

Visions Past
And Present

My Man Manuel .... *Page* 15

My Virginian .... *Page* 17

Vision of an Indian Headdress .... *Page* 18

My Friendly Tiger .... *Page* 20

Little People - or not? .... *Page* 22

The Xmas Tree that Played Wolf .... *Page* 24

Red Ferraris .... *Page* 25

From One Beach to Another .... *Page* 26

Visions of a Floating Suitcase .... *Page* 27

MY MAN MANUEL

A few months before Maggie's death, the face of a young man frequently appeared before me.

Faces often appear to me during meditation. Sometimes, too, when I close my eyes briefly, a face or a scene appears in full detail, just to the left of my eyes.

I often wonder why these scenes appear to the left rather than the right. The right side of the brain is the intuitive side, and yet all these appearances are to the left.

"My man", as I called this particular face, had sensitive dark eyes and longish dark hair.

Although his lips were thin, his cheeks and jaw were strong. He looked like a wistful dreamer and he smiled directly at me as if he knew a secret.

I was puzzled, not only as to who he was, but why he appeared so frequently.

Raymondo was taking a trip overseas, carrying Maggie's ashes to the place of her birth. I was to drive him to the airport.

As planned, we stopped off at his friend Graham's house for coffee. From here the three of us were to continue on. Graham is a high-profile music teacher and a caring friend to Raymondo.

Suddenly, a photograph caught my eye. It was a face I knew well - the face of my man!

"That's my man!" I cried. "That's the man who keeps appearing before me! The man I keep talking about."

"That is Man," replied Graham. "That is his name, it's short for Manuel. Man was my friend who died earlier this year."

The three of us sat in stunned silence.

Graham gave Manuel's photo to me as a gift, assuring me he had many more. It is here in the room with me as I write. I'm receiving a big smile from him at this very moment.

A photograph that actually smiles!

MY VIRGINIAN

Many faces appear to me. Some I come to know, some I don't.

For about two months before I left Australia to "read" in Los Angeles, and to attend a four-day workshop with Lazaris, another young man kept appearing before me.

I called this one "My Virginian". He could have stepped right out of a George Washington movie.

My Virginian had a body as well as a face, and I wondered if his Olde Worlde clothing held a special meaning.

I was soon to know.

The first day of the workshop with Lazaris arrived. About four hundred of us filled the room.

Suddenly from the other side of the crowd I noticed a man waving at me, trying to attract my attention.

"My Virginian"! In the flesh!

He pushed his way through the throng and came towards me with arms outstretched.

"I just have to give you a big hug," he cried.

"You're my Virginian," I exclaimed. "I've been seeing your face in my meditation for weeks."

"I *am* a Virginian - born and bred. I often move out here to the coast to live, but I no sooner arrive than I decide to high-tail it back to Virginia."

The Mystery of the Virginian was solved. From the visions of olde style clothing I believe he had a previous life in the state of Virginia.

VISION OF AN INDIAN HEADDRESS

Another time in California my son's face appeared during meditation. I remember thinking, "Now here's a face I know".

While I watched his face floating before me, the

fresh smell of pine trees wafted through the air-conditioned room.

I heard the muffled sound of pine needles crackling underfoot - in a room where every person was still.

The unmistakable sounds of a waterfall came into the conference room. I wondered if anyone else could hear them.

I marveled at just how detailed Sonny's face appeared. The same fair complexion and thick blond hair, the yellow eyebrows and yellow eyelashes that have not darkened with the years.

The details seemed magnified.

He made eye contact with my closed eyes, smiled, and then very slowly turned his head to the side.

A feathered headdress suddenly appeared on his head, covering the blond hair. A long headdress, it was almost waist length and the feathers appeared to be all the same size.

He raised one hand over his eyes and looked into the distance. Although his features didn't alter at all, he had the face of an Indian.

Strange as it may sound, Sonny has reddish skin in this lifetime.

When he was born my father looked at his new grandson in the hospital crib. "What an incredible coincidence," he exclaimed. "We've been born on the same day and month. Grandfather and grandson sharing the same day of birth. But I wonder why he has such red skin?"

I just know from this vision that my son has lived on American soil in another lifetime, as a Native American Indian.

MY FRIENDLY TIGER

The "floating" faces aren't always human. Sometimes the visions are of animal faces!

For about six months I watched the face of a tiger during meditation. Sometimes he appeared just as I was drifting off to sleep.

My tiger would gaze directly into my eyes. He never appeared to be unfriendly. I became fascinated by him and looked forward to seeing him.

Before the tiger's first appearance, a stray tabby cat had wandered into a Sydney preschool we were associated with. He was a young desexed male, about twelve months old.

The staff named him "Tiger".

For two years he lived there, and for two years the staff tried in vain to find a home for him.

We wanted to take him, but at that time had two elderly Siamese cats. Adult Siamese are quite elitist and would never accept a "moggie".

After they left this life, we were able give Tiger a home with us.

Kimbles, our red cattle dog, whimpered, then wagged her tail and rolled on the floor in submission. A dog's way of saying "welcome".

A familiar tap rapped on the back of my head and I knew I was about to receive a message. The message of "other lifetimes" came through to me.

Was this, then, the reason Kimbles and Tiger accepted each other so readily in this life?

One afternoon Tiger curled up on the couch next to me, positioning himself to face me directly.

He gently placed his head on my lap, gazed up at me and started to purr.

As I admired his beautiful stripes, I noticed his eyes becoming larger. His head began to grow and his stripes expanded.

I was awed to find the face of a large tiger in my lap, purring away and gazing at me with love.

The huge tiger and my tabby cat were one.

I know now he lived a lifetime in the body of that beautiful tiger.

I'm sure I knew him then.

The tiger face hasn't appeared since. I suppose there's no longer a need.

LITTLE PEOPLE - OR NOT?

Having faces appear during meditation is a common occurrence for me. But there are times when scenes, and people, "alter" without warning - and I just have to wait until they right themselves again.

Visiting our local medical center one morning, I was surprised to find a new doctor on duty. He told me he was in favor of hypnosis and meditation, and appeared to have an open mind.

As he talked about meditation, I suddenly became aware that this doctor was one of the "little people".

"It's strange that I didn't notice earlier," I thought, "when he opened the door, called my name and invited me into his surgery."

Within minutes, Doctor had changed on me. He was no longer a Little Person.

I was very confused.

However, I was to become even more confused.

Doctor now proceeded to change back and forth from an average height to that of a Little Person.

At one stage he started to swing his legs back and forth under the chair, as children do when their legs don't reach the floor.

I was amazed to see him write with a quilled pen.

Unfortunately my "changing" doctor didn't stay at the center. He suddenly moved to South Australia - just after assuring the other staff that he intended to stay permanently.

Because I have these visions regularly, I was not prepared for the vision of "the tree that would not change back."

THE XMAS TREE THAT PLAYED WOLF

It was the month of June and as I turned away from a counter in a large department store, I was confronted by a beautifully decorated Christmas tree.

A huge tree, shining and twinkling as only a Christmas tree can.

"This one can't be real!" I thought. "No way! Christmas is six months off. I will just wait a few moments until it disappears."

I waited and I waited.

The tree stayed put.

Here I was out-waiting a tree - and becoming later and later for a luncheon appointment.

"What a stubborn tree," I thought. "I've never had an object or scene take this long to change before."

I began to wonder if, maybe, the Christmas tree was real after all.

Throughout lunch, I puzzled over it's existence.

Later I returned to the tree with a friend - who confirmed that it did, in fact, exist. It was part of a "Christmas in Winter" promotion.

Here in Australia, Christmas falls in the heat of summer. Many restaurants have a field day during our coldest winter months of June and July, serving hot Christmas dinners to the traditionalists.

I wonder if this is the only country in the world to celebrate Christmas twice a year?

RED FERRARIS

On another occasion, my daughter and I were driving to Jandakot Airport in Perth, Western Australia, when

I became aware of a striking red Ferrari ahead of us.

We caught up and stayed behind it for quite some time. Finally I said, "Now that's what I call a car! Isn't that Ferrari outstanding?"

"What Ferrari?" she asked. And it disappeared before my eyes.

This was to be the beginning of many red Ferrari appearances and disappearances. They are here one moment in full detail; and in the time it takes to blink an eye, they no longer exist. I sometimes wonder what it's all about. Why do I "see" Ferraris?

FROM ONE BEACH TO ANOTHER

When scenery around me changes, it can be a little startling. Especially when I find myself in a different country, on the other side of the world.

As I walked along the Manhattan beach in California, I became aware that the scenery had suddenly changed.

I was now on a lonely beach near Perth. It was a beach I was familiar with, and just as deserted now as the last time I had been there.

One moment I was admiring the American coast - and in the blink of an eye I was halfway across the world, in Australia.

"Oh, oh!" I thought. "I wonder why this is happening. I must be in two places at once."

I stood perfectly still and waited for the scene to change back. I received a tap on the back of my head. The message "New California" came through.

Instantly, I was back on the busy beach in the USA. Walking along as if it was a normal, everyday event to change from one country to another and back again. And all within a few minutes.

Maybe Western Australia will be the new California!

VISIONS OF A FLOATING SUITCASE

For a short while a vision of a suitcase had me puzzled.

My birthday was approaching and my husband wanted to give me a gift of new luggage. For some time I had been "seeing" a suitcase - during meditation and often when I closed my eyes briefly.

It was a light-brown case with very wide straps - much wider than normal.

Paul had already shopped around and was familiar with the latest luggage. He now wanted me to choose from a selection he thought the most suitable.

I looked at the line of cases in the department store, closed my eyes briefly and the vision of the brown suitcase floated up before me.

"I really appreciate all the time and effort you've put into this project," I said to Paul. "However, I keep seeing the same brown suitcase and I really get 'No!' to choosing one at the moment."

"Okay," he replied. "If you think that has some significance, I will just have to come up with something else in place of luggage for you."

My birthday finally arrived.

I love birthdays. I'm a person who loves any excuse to celebrate life. I like to produce a carrot cake and ceremoniously cut and serve it to celebrate even a fun-filled day, or any satisfactory happening.

The doorbell rang and I hurried to answer it. On the doorstep stood my thoughtful son-in-law with a very large gift.

"Happy birthday!" he said. "It was hard to wrap."

Of course! The parcel contained the very same suitcase I had been seeing for weeks.

I believe most people experience similar happenings. Not everyone "views" the message they are receiving. Many would say they "think" the message.

Ever thought of a friend you haven't seen or heard from for some time, only to have them suddenly contact you?

How many times have you heard the phone ring and thought, "That's so and so", then find yourself saying, "I just knew it was you".

This usually happens when we take the first thought that comes into our head, instead of analyzing everything.

Our first thoughts flow from our intuition, and our intuition is always "spot on". It is only wishful thinking that can be wrong.

When we practice tuning into our intuition it can be rewarding and a lot of fun.

Only yesterday I was nearing an unfamiliar destination and had the choice of turning either left or right into a street.

As I approached the corner I thought, "I *think* I need to go left. But what would intuition say?"

Immediately I "got" the answer - "Right".

I turned right and, of course, intuition was correct.

Intuition, psychic ability, and "gut instinct" go hand in hand. In fact, I believe they are the same thing.

Detectives firmly believe in their "gut instinct". Most Detectives would be horrified to think that their "gut instinct" is also their psychic ability.

CHAPTER THREE

MESSAGES FROM BEYOND

A Father's Visit . . . . *Page* 34

A Visit from Lazaris . . . . *Page* 37

Askor's Message . . . . *Page* 40

Silzaar's Message . . . . *Page* 41

I lose the information I receive during a Reading, just as quickly as I've received it. Clients phone me back the same day and I can't recall any information at all.

Many Readers will tell you they become spaced out during a Reading and need to limit the number of clients they see each day.

The spaced-out feeling comes as the state of consciousness alters, to a level not unlike the dream state. When we awaken from a dream, we can remember most of it. But as we come slowly into a wide-awake state, memory of the dream fades.

This also happens with readings. I tend to lose all memory of a Reading after I emerge from that dreamlike state and come out of trance.

I have been known to read for twelve people in one day, and then happily go on to do a six-hour time slot on radio.

This includes taking over a hundred calls from listeners; interviewing astrologers, hypnotherapists, and so on; as well as doing live "reads" for commercials.

And all the time working from a state of trance. My husband believes I am constantly in a state of trance.

Do I have a problem with that?

No! I just love being in trance.

There is, however, one Reading I will never forget.

A FATHER'S VISIT

My client was a pretty girl with an animated face. She nodded in agreement with every word I said.

"That's right! That's right!" she repeated over and over, in confirmation.

Suddenly "Identikit" eyes appeared in place of her own.

The eyes of my father!

My dad had left this life years before, and now his eyes were smiling into mine as if he'd never gone.

I was instantly out of my body, looking down from the ceiling, watching the two of us in conversation. Somehow the Reading kept going. I was actually observing myself talking and my client nodding.

My father's eyes were shining and laughing with sheer delight. I could see the crinkles at the corners of his eyes, and every eyelash in full detail. My dad's name was Gordon Pemberton and I repeatedly "got" the name Pemberton. But even though I was being tapped sharply on the back of the head, I held back from saying it.

"Not now Dad! Not now!" I silently implored. I thought the message must surely be for me, not for my client.

However, the more I tried to hold back, the stronger the tapping on my head became.

Finally I said, "Pemberton! I am 'getting' the name Pemberton around you."

"I can't believe you said that! I can't believe you picked that up!"

The message was for her. It really was for her!

I was instantly back in my body. The Identikit eyes were gone, but not so my father. I could feel his delight and happiness. Zigzags appeared in the air all around me.

"Whow!" I thought. "If only she knew how I picked that one up!"

My body was tingling from head to toe. The air around me seemed to be moving along with the zigzags.

"Feeling" my father's laughter was an incredible experience. His words "yes! yes!" were audible and clear. They filled the room, but I knew I was the only one hearing him.

When the Reading was over I immediately phoned my nephew Pan. He was the only family member, apart from my husband and children, that I could share the excitement with.

Pan is a psychic. He is also a homeopath and teacher of meditation. Of course, he was thrilled to hear the news of his grandfather's involvement in my Reading.

A VISIT FROM LAZARIS

Then there was my unforgettable personal experience with Lazaris. Lazaris can be very loving and also very funny.

Early one evening I listened to his tapes as I cooked the evening meal. (I call Lazaris "him" when, in fact, he is neither male nor female.)

I doubled over with laughter at an outrageously funny remark he made.

"Lazaris! Lazaris!" I cried aloud. "I can't believe you said that! I can't believe that came from you. I love you Lazaris, I really, really do."

Here I was laughing and crying at the same time. It took a while to recover.

It was amazing to think that an entity could have such a sense of humor!

Meal preparation over, I switched the tape off and sat down, still smiling broadly, to reflect on Lazaris' statement.

A wave of what could only be described as sheer love hit me. It surged through my body, engulfing me completely.

The surge continued on and on. Time seemed to stand still.

Love was all that existed. I knew, beyond doubt, that it was Lazaris.

Much later, Paul came downstairs and found me with tears streaming down my face.

"Lazaris was here!" I explained.

Some months later, I attended a four-day intensive workshop with Lazaris in Los Angeles.

At the end of the four days, each person spends a few personal moments with this loving entity.

People carry their crystals to Lazaris to have them charged with energy.

The very experience of waiting is awesome. Standing in line to speak with him is an amazing experience. You can actually feel the love in the room.

As each person reaches Lazaris, they tell him their name. He apparently tunes into its vibration.

I understand this - I use the same method during a Reading . When someone wants to know about somebody else, I ask them to, "Say their first name a few times for me". Then suddenly I've tuned into the vibration and can proceed to tell my client all about the owner of the name.

I said, "It's Dawn Rawlings, Lazaris."

Instantly the reply came. "Oh! Dawn, we really did enjoy visiting with you."

I started to laugh. "Lazaris, thank you for visiting; and Lazaris, thank you so much for remembering."

Lazaris smiled broadly through his Channel. "And Dawn, we really, really, do love you too!"

I still smile to myself about this incredible experience.

Incredible that the very words I had called out, months before from my home in Australia, were fed back to me in Los Angeles by Lazaris, an entity who has never lived on the earth.

A truly unforgettable experience!

A similar incident occurred with the Light Being, Askor, who channels through Chris Power of Australia.

ASKOR'S MESSAGE

While Chris and I were lecturing at the Newport Spiritual Expo in Sydney's northern beaches area, he suggested that I might enjoy a session with Askor.

Of course, I was delighted.

Askor came through with greetings and love. Next he informed me of the bright colors of light coming from my third eye.

I was fine until he began to praise me.

"Oh, oh!" I thought. "I'd better tune into this to make sure Askor is for real."

Immediately a blast of cold air hit the back of my neck. I turned around to see who the culprit was.

There was not a soul in sight!

I turned back to face the Channel. Askor said, "Just letting you know I'm real, Dawn."

I no longer had any doubts at all.

SILZAAR'S MESSAGE

One other time, we were having our usual Thursday night channel session at home with Silzaar, another channeled and loving entity.

Lisa Joyce of Sydney is the channel for Silzaar.

Lisa had gone into trance and Silzaar was now speaking directly to me.

I mentioned some details of my future plans to Silzaar. He replied, "It's all in the cards, Dawn."

I was puzzled at first, then realized that he was referring to *The Crystal Cards*. At the time I was busy with the design and production of these highly accurate prediction cards.

Silzaar also has a sense of humor.

CHAPTER FOUR

BELIEFS

Three Score Years and Ten .... *Page 47*

A Change of Luck .... *Page 48*

Same Life - Different Illusion .... *Page 54*

A List of Speakers .... *Page 57*

Trancing on National TV .... *Page 61*

A Loaf of Bread .... *Page 63*

The Red Barbecue Story .... *Page 66*

*All you have on the earth plane are
your beliefs. Nothing else exists.*
- **Roemann**

*At no time are events predestined.
With every moment you change
and every action changes every other action.*
- **Seth**

I always tell friends and clients that I'm not a "doom and gloom" Reader. I believe we all create our own futures, our own realities, regardless of circumstances.

Therefore, when I see something I don't like in someone's future, I believe it's important to let them know that I'm seeing the future which they, themselves, are creating.

They alone are creating their future and they are always free to change it.

Whenever I make a decision to change a project or alter the direction I've been taking in life, I am amazed to notice the difference in the lines of the palms of my hands. The "Fate or karma" showing up in our palms has been chosen entirely by ourselves.

We always have choice. Our entire future is formed from our beliefs and expectations.

I once heard Louise Hay say during a lecture, "I know you don't like me to tell you that you create your own reality, even though you do."

Louise is so right!

Many of us would rather believe that something outside our control is responsible for the mess we've made of our lives, rather than our own beliefs.

We've all heard the quote, "What we eat today, walks and talks tomorrow".

My belief is, "What we believe today, walks and talks tomorrow".

THREE SCORE YEARS AND TEN

My parents were Jehovah's Witnesses in this lifetime. My father a fanatical one.

He repeatedly quoted, "The Lord gives us three score year and ten, that's all the Lord gives us. We are not meant to live past seventy years. That's all the Lord allows us."

I used to tell him that he was, in fact, affirming that he should only live to seventy. "You will go at seventy Dad, if you keep feeding that belief into your subconscious mind," I warned.

"Many people live a lot longer than seventy, but you tell yourself every day that you should only live to that age."

I might add that my father carried his birth certificate in his wallet. He delighted in having people guess his age. At seventy he didn't look a day over forty-five. His face was unlined and he had a full head of black curly hair. I can't ever remember him walking, as most folk do. He always ran!

My father's death must have been a Jehovah's Witnesses' dream come true!

Brother Hector Gordon Pemberton dropped dead after returning from church one Sunday, as he stood in his bedroom Reading the Bible.

He was three score year and ten!

A CHANGE OF LUCK

There are people in life who insist on affirming, "I never have any luck!" or "I will never get out of debt".

The funny, or sad, part about it is: they are absolutely right. They do not attract good luck and, of course, they remain in debt.

While they continue to feed this information into their subconscious mind, their life remains unaltered.

I have a regular client who constantly used to tell me, "I am always the unlucky one" or "I know it's too good to be true".

He really was experiencing a long period of "bad luck". He had just come through a bitter divorce and was struggling to keep his business afloat. The house he had finished paying for had been lost in the divorce.

The mother he loved so much had passed away twelve months ago, not long after marrying a very caring man - a man who provided her with a beautiful home and wanted to spend the rest of his life making her happy.

"I knew it was too good to be true," he explained to me at the time of her death.

After knowing a brutal father earlier in life, he had grown very close to his stepfather.

And the reason he had come to me today was out of sadness and despair. His stepfather, too, had died quietly in his sleep.

During the session I received a sharp tap on the back of my head and I suddenly realized that I had just asked him a question, "Do you believe in the Law of Averages?"

He said, "Of course I do! Everyone knows it exists."

"Well is there any reason you couldn't believe, based on the Law of Averages, that tomorrow could be slightly different? That maybe, just for one day, some luck could show up for you?"

"Just for tomorrow?" he asked tentatively.

"I'm not asking you to expect the luck to last more than one day. Take your time and think about it."

After a lot of thought, he said, "Yeah! Just for one day. Of course! I could be lucky for one day only. I know it wouldn't last for any longer than that though."

The stage was set!

I gave him a pad and pen and asked him to write down his beliefs about yesterday. His beliefs about what he had expected to happen.

Next I asked him to check to see if, in fact, his beliefs had proved correct.

And indeed they had!

For yesterday he had written, "I believed that it would be just another lousy day".

On checking the outcome, he had added "I was one hundred percent right".

I then asked him to write down what his beliefs about tomorrow were, prior to seeing me today.

Again he wrote, "Another lousy day".

"Are your beliefs still the same?" I asked. "Do you still expect a lousy day?"

He thought it over for a few moments, smiled, then proceeded to cross out his words.

"Now we are getting somewhere," I said. "Why don't you write your new beliefs about tomorrow and put the date on it?"

Without hesitation he bent over the notepad and wrote...

"**1.** This day could be my lucky day.

2. Some luck could come into my life."

He warmed to the possibilities.

"**3.** Tomorrow is my lucky day. Tomorrow is my lucky day."

Why not write "I am lucky now?" I coached. "Why not write it a few times?"

The almost instant change in him amazed me. He jumped to his feet and paced the room as he made decisions about buying a few lottery tickets and also a lotto entry.

I suggested that I work out his birth numbers for luck.

I also told him to expect luck to come from other sources, apart from the lottery.

From places unknown and unexpected.

From places he is not even aware of.

To let miracles happen.

"Of course it will come from anywhere," he agreed. "If tomorrow is my lucky day, then luck could come from anywhere at all."

Together we wrote out his affirmations. He put them in his pocket, eager to chant them repeatedly later.

As he left, I knew he now expected that luck could show up.

Expecting is much more powerful than hoping and wishing.

He remarked that he was tingling all over and really looking forward to his lucky day.

"This Law of Averages is real, you know. It's something I really believe in. And everyone knows it exists!" This was his parting remark.

I wondered if I had created a monster.

I find myself smiling as I recall the outcome.

He didn't win a huge amount of money. He won five hundred dollars.

However, he did receive a letter informing him that his stepfather, who had no other relatives, had bequeathed him his beautiful home, filled with antiques, plus his car.

Day one of his new beliefs!

I wonder, too, what the outcome would have been if he hadn't taken conscious control of his beliefs.

Would it have been "just another lousy day"?

SAME LIFE - DIFFERENT ILLUSION

A young relative of mine is a God-fearing Jehovah's Witness. We meet occasionally for coffee and a chat.

In her belief, the world around us is becoming "increasingly evil and wicked" as each day passes. The devil exists for her and at the moment, for some unknown reason, he has more power than God.

She hasn't noticed that Russia and the USA are now on friendly terms.

Equality manifested in South Africa and she didn't even notice.

While I celebrated these events, peace talks came to Northern Ireland, and Israel and Jordan signed a peace agreement. She still didn't notice.

In my illusion the world is improving at a rapid rate - and I can prove it. In her illusion violence and despair are all that exists - and she can prove that.

You may ask, "Who is right?"

The answer is both! For life is only an illusion. An illusion formed entirely from our own beliefs.

In this Monumental decade, miracles are happening. We are watching history being written.

On the 23rd of April 1994, our Earth linked with the star Sirius. It has been ninety-thousand years since we last connected with Sirius. And it will be another ninety-thousand years before it happens again.

The Vortex of Sirius opened, resulting in the emergence of the Goddess energy. This is a softer energy, a peaceful energy.

The Earth receives a "booster" on the 23rd of each month during this decade, and we are reaping the results.

Whatever we concentrate on at this time intensifies. The results come at a rapid rate. If we concentrate on problems and doom and gloom, then problems and doom and gloom will certainly intensify.

However, if we concentrate on just how good it will be when a solution drops in from out of the blue, then the solution will take on the intensity instead.

I have fun working with my beliefs. Each evening, I simply write down the beliefs I have about the next day.

This makes me aware of what I believe, and it is amazing to realize just how limiting our beliefs are at times.

If I am not happy with what I've written, I then write down what I'd like to believe about tomorrow.

Next I ask myself, "Is there any reason I can't believe this about tomorrow?"

I suppose it is all a matter of processing.

If you find you have limiting beliefs, that's fine! Congratulate yourself for recognizing the fact, and use it to your advantage.

Write down your new beliefs, and have fun achieving all you consciously expect daily.

A LIST OF SPEAKERS

Recently I attended a special seminar in Sydney. The speakers included Michael Domeyko Rowland, Dr Wayne Dyer, Louise Hay, Marianne Williamson and Stuart Wilde.

The day was Thursday. The seminar was on from nine to five.

My weekly segment on national television, the "At Home Show" with John Mangos, is taped each Thursday. My usual call time is around four-thirty.

I would be able to attend the lectures. However, I would have to miss the last speaker, and Marianne Williamson was scheduled last.

On Wednesday evening as I wrote down my beliefs about the day ahead, I realized just how disappointed I felt about missing Marianne.

I also became aware that I expected a hassle with having to rush off to the "At Home Show". I realized that I expected to arrive in a flurry and be hassled about the whole thing.

The subject of my segment that day was Past Lives.

I prefer to put people back into past lives with hypnosis. They then do all the talking.

They tell of the life they are experiencing, the country they are living in, their name; and they sometimes know the actual date.

They are also aware of their culture, family, friends and occupation.

The information given by a client under hypnosis is extremely comprehensive and as I am not in trance myself, I am able to remember it if necessary.

However, when I am asked to "pick up" past lives on someone who is absent, the method I use is entirely different.

I call these "Permission Past Lives". I ask permission of the person's Higher Self (I usually use my channel board for this). If permission is granted, I then go into trance and watch the scenes that float around me.

There is, however, a drawback with this method.

Because trancing is similar to the dream state, the information can be lost as you move back into a normal state of consciousness. One must write everything down before the memory becomes obscure.

On this occasion, I had gone into trance several days beforehand for the information I needed. I would certainly need time to look at my notes before going on camera.

I would be running late. Would I have time?

The Prime Minister of Australia was to be my main subject.

In my journal I had written, "I would like to believe that I will be calm and relaxed and have instant recall of all past lives, resulting in an enjoyable and successful segment."

Because I would need to leave the lecture early, I had also written that a miracle would take place, allowing me to hear all the speakers I needed to hear.

In brackets I had written, "If a speaker is missed, let it be one I can catch up with in the near future".

We arrived for the start of "Success Congress '94" along with a crowd of four thousand other enthusiastic people.

I waved to Leon Nacson, publisher of *The Planet* newspaper and co-ordinator of the Congress, and we stopped to chat. During the course of our conversation Leon mentioned that Marianne Williamson had been unavoidably detained in America and would be joining the tour in Perth.

I was astounded.

"Leon, why don't you take her place and talk about your dream book, *The Dreamer's Guide to the Galaxy?*"

"I would love to one day but I don't think it's appropriate right now. I'm sure the audience would appreciate hearing more from Louise, Wayne and Stuart."

Suddenly guilt reared its ugly head...

Had I created the absence of Marianne? Had my affirmations and beliefs been responsible? I agonized over the thought.

No! This wouldn't make sense.

I had believed that if I missed a speaker, it would be one I could hear in the near future - and Marianne certainly doesn't make a habit of coming to Australia.

I had expected a miracle, and a miracle it would be!

Louise Hay and Dr Wayne Dyer extended their talks, and Stuart Wilde became the last speaker.

Unfortunately, I did miss his lecture that day. However, Stuart is frequently in Australia and I would be able to see him shortly.

Events seemed to be working out after all.

TRANCING ON NATIONAL TV

On arrival at the "At Home Show", I was hurried through make-up and hair, and onto the set.

John Mangos, the show's host, is a warm and wonderful Cancer, blessed with good looks and the ability to make his guests feel completely relaxed.

He is, however, a little skeptical concerning metaphysical matters.

John and I exchanged friendly greetings. He then asked me about the past lives of our Prime Minister, Paul Keating.

As I had not had time to look at my notes, I quickly "asked" to recall the experience.

I started to speak, and suddenly felt myself trancing. I certainly wanted to recall the information - but not through trance!

I was so spaced out, I could hardly put two words together.

Scenes from Northern Ireland floated past, complete with Spanish freedom fighters.

I remember wondering where on earth Mr Keating was.

As I fought to keep my eyes open, one of the fighters turned around and looked straight into my eyes.

I had found him.

Mr Paul Keating was a Spanish freedom fighter in Northern Ireland in a past life!

I was still in trance and fighting to bring myself out. Although it seemed to take forever, apparently it didn't.

During the same segment I started to trance again, but managed to take control instantly.

As I left the set, one of the crew remarked, "Good segment, Dawn!" I smiled and breathed a sigh of relief. This had been a hair-raising experience and one I wouldn't want to go through again.

Why? Because, deep down, I really didn't believe I could recall dream-state past lives without trance.

My beliefs had created the outcome of the day.

A LOAF OF BREAD

Two friends of mine do believe in being conscious of their daily beliefs. They affirm positive affirmations and are aware of their thoughts throughout the day.

Lately, Chris decided to leave his managerial position. His aim was to find a new position in a more positive environment.

Although this meant living on his wife's part-time income, they trusted in their belief that they would somehow be able to pay each bill as it came in.

Their aim was to create a positive day, every day.

The weeks passed and they were managing quite well. But only just! There was never a cent to spare.

Were they believing that survival at the basic level was the only way to go?

After buying the groceries one morning, they realized they'd forgotten to buy a loaf of bread. They also realized that there wasn't enough money left to pay for one.

Lisa really enjoyed a slice of bread and always chose her favorite, a white high-fiber loaf.

At first a few negative thoughts crept in, but these were soon canceled. They'd managed to pay each bill as it came in, so there was no reason to believe that the creation of a loaf of bread would be an impossible achievement.

Late that evening, the couple went for their usual walk around the neighborhood and found - yes, a loaf of bread.

Not only a loaf of bread, but a completely sealed loaf of white high-fiber, "starring" at midnight on the footpath in suburban Cherrybrook.

They told me their story with great excitement. I laughed as I visualized them dancing around and jumping up and down with glee under the street light.

I could almost hear their laughter and shouts of excitement. A miracle had been created by them that night.

A miracle that evolved entirely from their expectations and beliefs.

I wonder how many miracles they will create in their future, now they really know the secret of manifesting?

When they shared this event with me, I realized that Lisa hadn't concentrated on the absence of bread in her life at all. Her focus had been on expecting and believing that she would have it.

A few weeks later, Chris manifested his new job. He now holds a highly paid position in a positive environment, and describes his boss as "the nicest man I have ever worked for".

I told the story of the loaf of bread to Shane, who owns the Elements of Nature crystal shop in the Rocks area of Sydney.

Shane laughed heartily and said, "It's very similar to my red barbecue story".

THE RED BARBECUE STORY

Shane's friends had planned a Saturday evening party to celebrate their engagement. Shane had promised to buy them the small red barbecue they wanted.

He had also promised to bring it on the night of the party, as they planned to cook the sautés on it.

"I left the buying to the last minute, ran around to every outlet - and couldn't find a small red barbie anywhere," Shane explained.

He bought an alternative gift and went home to get ready for the evening.

Before leaving for the party, he decided to give his dogs a run in the back laneway.

His thoughts were on a small red barbecue and just how much his friends would appreciate one. He was, in fact, concentrating on "the having" - not "the lack of".

As he opened the gate, he was confronted by the sight of a brand new red barbecue standing alone in the laneway. The same one he had tried in vain to buy.

Not a soul in sight, just a new red barbecue!

Was he dreaming? No! He knew it wasn't a dream.

A miracle had happened!

Where did it come from? Shane remembers "looking left and right and then only up". The Universe had provided!

The barbecue was hastily gift-wrapped and taken to the party, where it proved a huge success.

Days later, Shane listened in amazement as his neighbor told how her husband had driven the car around to the back lane and loaded in the children, the picnic hamper, beach umbrella, and so on, before the family happily drove off to enjoy a picnic in the park.

On arrival, the car was unpacked. Their barbecue, it seems, had mysteriously disappeared.

They were mystified, but decided it was all for the best as they needed a larger one anyway!

Shane told them of the miracle of finding, in the laneway, the very barbecue he needed - apparently their lost barbecue! He also offered a contribution towards their new one.

CHAPTER FIVE

Adventures Of A Meditator

An Affinity with Spiders .... *Page* 73

The Causal Plane .... *Page* 75

A Sense of Taste .... *Page* 78

Non-existent Flowers .... *Page* 79

Our state of consciousness not only alters with hypnosis, sleep and the dream state, but also when we "doze off" or daydream.

And, of course, it alters with meditation!

Many folk believe they are too uptight to meditate. If this were true, most of us would miss out completely.

In fact, I find that the more uptight I am, the more urgent the need for me to meditate.

Meditation works regardless of how stressed we are. Maybe *because* of how stressed we are.

When we meditate we go within. And, of course, all knowledge is within. Meditation is a way of touching base with our inner self, our Higher Self, and also with our soul.

During meditation we are in touch with who we really are - we "go home" so to speak.

Meditation is one of my delights in life.

With my busy schedule I have to give it top priority, otherwise it gets left out. Everything else has to fit around it.

I rise early and meditate before I start my day. Then around four each afternoon, I hang out the "Do Not Disturb" sign, turn the answering machine on and, once again, "go home".

Time-consuming, you may ask?

Perhaps. But the benefits are endless. I seem to accomplish so much more. Energy levels and vitality stay high. Everyday hassles seem minor rather than major.

I have learned many "types" of meditation. You may choose to meditate with a mantra or a breathing technique, or maybe both. The colors of the chakras might also become a favorite.

When I learned an advanced Sidhis technique, I needed to spend two weeks on a farm in Victoria, one of Australia's cooler states, during the winter season.

The buildings were made of mud brick. The very basic accommodation could best be described as rustic.

Although I enjoyed the program and food immensely, I didn't enjoy retiring each evening to a lonely mud-brick room, complete with cowpats on the wall.

"I definitely do not have an affinity with cow-pats," I told myself. I didn't realize that I was soon to have an affinity with a spider!

AN AFFINITY WITH SPIDERS

It was cold in Victoria and one night, after a hot shower, I quickly reached for the pair of thick flannelette PJ's I'd borrowed from Paul. As I thrust one leg in, a huge black spider was kicked out unceremoniously onto the earthen floor.

I sensed his thoughts immediately. His indignation seemed to rise up to meet me.

His thoughts weren't down on the floor where his physical body was. They were level with my face, and I felt his emotions as clearly as he must have felt them himself.

He was not pleased at all. I had physically kicked him out of his bed.

I found myself apologizing out loud to the spider for the assault and inconvenience. "I am so sorry, I'm just so sorry," I repeated again and again.

I "felt" and "heard" him stamp away.

It was an uncanny experience and I have had an affinity with spiders ever since. I just know when one has fallen into the pool at home - and, of course, I go out and rescue it.

I know it is not uncommon to have an affinity with insects or flowers when one learns to meditate.

My affinity just happens to be with spiders and I don't have an answer as to why.

When meditating, I sometimes experience an extremely light feeling, as if my body were weightless. I often reach a blissful state of incredible peace and happiness.

I have learned from experience that it is essential to come out of the meditative state slowly, to avoid becoming agitated.

To come out quickly is a little like being shaken out of a deep sleep.

If this ever happens, I just take deep breaths, and go back in for a few moments. I concentrate on slowly opening my eyes, slowly stretching, and allowing myself to focus properly before moving around.

THE CAUSAL PLANE

One of my favorite meditations is on an audio cassette tape, "The Causal Plane" meditation by Lazaris (from the "Manifesting What You Want" series).

I love to turn the tape on and sit with my eyes closed, allowing Lazaris to lead me to the Causal plane where cause and effect take place.

The meditation is very relaxing and visual.

In it he describes the trees and shrubs as angular in shape, the colors of the sky and the grass as different to those on the Earth plane.

At first I found the angular shapes hard to imagine. I found myself thinking how I much preferred the soft, round shapes of our trees and shrubs.

That is until the day I experienced the angular ones.

As I drove through an adjoining suburb one bright sunny day, I admired the familiar leafy area and slowed down to cross a small bridge over a creek.

Our local agricultural showground adjoins this scenic, semi-rural area. It was a road I'd traveled many, many times before.

Today however, it was different!

The whole landscape was angular in appearance. The shrubs as well as the trees were angular instead of round or oval.

And yet the change seemed completely normal.

"Lazaris is right! The trees really are angular! They really are!" I cried aloud.

I continued to admire the scene for some time.

By the time I reached home however, the landscape had returned to normal.

And as I looked at my predominantly native garden, I felt a little sad because the trees in my driveway were not angular like those in the adjoining neighborhood of Castle Hill.

I sat in the car, reliving the amazing experience of the different shapes.

Suddenly I felt a tap on the back of my head and I welcomed the signal of a message coming through. "The Causal plane is only an altered state away" the message stated.

"How true! how true!" I responded. "How very, very true!"

Now when I listen to the soft "voice" of Lazaris as he guides me through the Causal plane meditation, I have no trouble visualizing the angular shapes at all. I simply allow my thoughts to go directly to my bridge and the bushland at Castle Hill.

A SENSE OF TASTE

I remember feeling drowsy while Reading *Out On A Limb*, one of Shirley MacLaine's best-selling books.

An entity who had lived the life of an Irish pickpocket was channeling through a psychic in order to talk directly to Shirley.

As I read of his conversation with her, I felt myself beginning to trance. Because of this I decided to take a break and have a quick snack for lunch.

I hastily put some leftover peas and carrots into the microwave oven to heat, aware of just how uninteresting the meal looked.

But as I started to eat I found myself with the most sumptuous meal I had ever experienced. It was unbelievably delicious.

I couldn't remember a more appetizing dish.

"This is like a banquet, the flavor is out of this world. We must have carrots and peas more often," I decided as I headed back to the kitchen for a second helping.

I was now aware that my feet were no longer touching the floor. This didn't concern me - the succulent feast awaited.

Much later, when I'd "come back to earth", I realized that my level of consciousness must have altered as I absorbed the words of the pickpocket.

This would have caused my senses to be heightened.

My sense of taste had certainly been heightened to the extreme.

NON-EXISTENT FLOWERS

When I first commenced a regular pattern of Meditation,(morning and afternoon) it was my sense of smell that became heightened. For no apparent reason, I would become aware of the strong fragrance of flowers.

This happened almost anytime, without any warning, whether or not there were flowers involved.

At first I would exclaim, "Oh, smell the flowers! Isn't the fragrance wonderful?" And then find people looking at me in amazement and saying, "What flowers? I can't smell any flowers!"

I soon learned to ask, "Can you smell flowers?" and make no other comment. "Just to be on the safe side", as my grandmother used to say.

This heightened sense has stayed with me for years. When I'm drifting off to sleep, I often smell the fragrance of flowers that are not of this world.

Just another delightful adventure in the life of a meditator!

CHAPTER SIX

CHANNEL-BOARD ADVENTURES

The Illusion of Psychic Attack .... *Page* 83

The Not-So-Merry Widow .... *Page* 85

Friends from the Other Side .... *Page* 87

The Hanging Judge .... *Page* 90

An Aspect of One's Self .... *Page* 91

Silzaar and Lisa .... *Page* 91

Mistaken Identity .... *Page* 93

The Goddess Isis .... *Page* 94

Uncle Harry Visits .... *Page* 100

THE ILLUSION OF PSYCHIC ATTACK

Often during a lecture or workshop, someone will mention a vision that has appeared to them. They are usually either thrilled, or afraid of their experience.

I know that fear only comes when it is invited, for fear is not a usual part of this illusion of life.

When I am in fear of anything - yes, even dreading tomorrow is a fear - I say in a positive, commanding manner, "Fear, I am no longer inviting you and I'm telling you to go".

And it works! Fear does only come when we invite it and it does go, as soon as we tell it to. For fear is not a normal emotion. It only exists if we bring it into our illusion.

When I hold workshops on developing psychic ability, or on using channel boards, I suggest that the same should apply to any vision we don't feel comfortable with.

Simply instruct any unwanted vision, feeling or entity to go.

But do take command. Don't be wishy-washy about it.

Many people ask me, "How do you protect yourself against psychic attack when using a channel board?"

I was just five years old when I first used the letters of the alphabet as my first channel board. Because I talk to so many entities on the board, people expect me to have hundreds of stories of psychic attack.

I don't. I don't have one - not even one little story to tell you.

Incidentally, Jane Roberts, author of *Seth Speaks*, met Seth on her Ouija board and I have no recollection of Jane ever experiencing psychic attack.

Now I know that some people will tell you the dreaded psychic attack does exist, that it is real!

And of course it is real, if you bring it into your illusion. But only if you bring it into your illusion.

I have never had any desire to talk to low-level entities and I don't choose to be involved with any.

THE NOT-SO-MERRY WIDOW

On one occasion when Maria, a newly widowed friend, and I were using the channel board, her deceased husband came through unexpectedly and uninvited.

His name was hastily spelled out, along with the message to "give her home to the eldest son". Maria's face turned white with anger.

I didn't waste a second! I barked the command "Go! And don't ever come back!"

I then turned to her and quietly remarked on the unusual way his name had been spelled out. "He must have spelled it incorrectly," I said.

"Oh no, he didn't!" Maria said. "That's the way his name is spelled."

Psychic attack does not exist in my illusion. It never has and it never will.

Life is not real. It is an illusion, our own illusion. Life appears differently to each of us. This is why we often have different opinions on different subjects.

Our very own beliefs and expectations create our lives, and our lives are an illusion.

The term "psychic attack" was formed originally to instill fear into people, in order to stop them searching.

Sadly, even today, many organizations control their population or members with fear.

To me it's reminiscent of the Boogeyman or the Devil, of a God that judges, of Hell or Satan.

I have a relative who warns against meditation, fearing "something slipping in and taking over", during the deep state of relaxation.

I sometimes wonder how she ever goes to sleep at night. She prays to Jesus to protect her against the evils of meditation and wine.

I know she has never indulged in a glass of wine in her life. So why indulge in the fear? Why invite the fear of wine?

I wonder, too, how she comes to terms with Jesus. Not only did Jesus spend time in meditation but, horror of horrors, Jesus also drank wine. And not only that, he actually turned water to wine at a wedding! And yet her beliefs ban wine from weddings.

FRIENDS FROM THE OTHER SIDE

Channel-board nights at home are nights of friendship, fun and hilarity.

Friendship, fun and hilarity with others who are not in a human body.

We talk to many who were not well-known during their lifetimes. To some who were household names, screen legends, philosophers and spiritual leaders. We talk to many who have never lived on the Earth plane at all.

Apparently this physical life is not the only place where one can develop and stretch and grow. It can be done on other dimensions and planes as well.

I talk to entities or personalities by invitation only. Sometimes an entity will mention that a friend of theirs would like to talk to me. This can be the start of a positive new friendship.

And so the list of friendships grows.

My mother May who left this life some years ago, is a channel-board friend. On my board, I've drawn a heart surrounded by flowers and written the name "May" in the heart.

We talk often on my channel board. It was during one of our talks that she requested a heart be drawn around her name.

My mother said, "Don't call me Mum or Mother between lives. Call me May. I've been a mother to thousands over many lifetimes. I'm not your mother between lives, I am your friend. Why don't we come back as girlfriends and have some fun together?"

May was born under the sign of Leo in this life. When I sense or see her during a consultation, I know she has a message about a Leo or someone named May.

Among the permanent names on my channel board is John; my Gateway; who puts me in touch with everyone. Providing, of course, that they want to be in touch with me.

Then there is Roemann; the Goddess Isis; Seth; Skye, our beautiful Doberman who shared her life with us; and Sam, Sebbie and Josh - Siamese cats who each spent a lifetime with us.

I also talk to Robert, my financial guide, and to my Guardian Angel.

Also to Matthew, a young friend of ours from this life, who tells us he was known as the Hanging Judge in the 1800's in the United States.

THE HANGING JUDGE

Matthew told us he chose this time around to experience "a short life on the wrong side of the law".

When I asked why, he answered, "To experience the other side of life. I'd always been intolerant of anyone who broke the law, and judged them harshly.

"As part of my spiritual growth, I decided to be on the receiving end of some harsh judgment for a change."

Of course, I asked if he would care to do it again. His reply was "No way, Dawn, no way!"

And no wonder! Our friend had only reached the age of thirty when he was blasted to death after an evening with some of his usual "companions".

As a clairvoyant I know that two people were involved in the shooting and not one. The person who fired the second shot, the fatal shot, has never been suspected at all, let alone charged with the crime.

Our departed friend tells us, via the channel board, that he couldn't care less about revenge. He chose to come back to Earth for the experience, and he accomplished that.

"End of story, Dawn, end of story," he tells me.

AN ASPECT OF ONE'S SELF

My husband talks to an aspect of himself. Yes! An aspect of himself who is a female writer in another country, during this parallel lifetime.

One could describe an aspect as "another self of one's self".

Contacts made with a parallel lifetime can be rewarding and even quite humorous.

We have so much fun contacting through the channel board and experience so much love!

SILZAAR AND LISA

Lisa, a client who has become a dear friend, joined our channel-board nights and her husband, Chris, came too. He originally came to talk to my financial guide, Robert, and this contact proved a great success.

Robert has become Chris' spirit guide as well as his financial guide. Seems those two shared a past life together as father and son.

Lisa's story is not unlike Jane Roberts' successful channeling of Seth.

Lisa met Silzaar, a loving high-level consciousness who had asked permission to converse with her on the channel board.

She spent days, weeks and months conversing with Silzaar on the board. He helped her emotionally and taught her to have confidence in herself.

One day Silzaar asked Lisa if she would like to verbally channel him.

Because of the quality of the information given by Silzaar during the many months of conversing together, Lisa was thrilled at the prospect.

She is an amazing channel - one of the best I have heard. Silzaar's messages are so positive and informative.

I notice that all the high-level entities have the same basic message: that we do create our own realities and that life is an illusion of whatever we perceive it to be.

I am lucky enough to converse frequently with Silzaar as he channels through Lisa. This has brought evenings filled with fun and love into my life.

Lisa and Silzaar are yet another triumph for using a channel board in a positive manner.

MISTAKEN IDENTITY

It is the norm in our home to have a channeling event happening in one room and, at the same time, a hypnosis session taking place in another.

Paul and fellow hypnotherapist Anthony are involved in hypnosis research together.

Anthony doesn't understand channeling and had never been exposed to it. In fact, he never believed in hypnosis before learning Neuro-Linguistic Programming.

One night he and Paul finished their session early and Anthony hurried in to say goodbye to everyone.

He didn't realize we were in the middle of a channel session with Silzaar.

Anthony spoke loudly to us and then turned to Lisa who, of course, was in a deep state of trance. "Good night! See you next week," he said.

Now Silzaar has a completely different "voice" and "accent" (for want of better words) to his channel, Lisa Joyce.

But Silzaar didn't miss a beat. "And a very good evening to you Anthony. It will be a pleasure to see you again next week," he answered.

Telly Savalis is a channel-board friend. He narrated the "Channeling from Beyond" tape during this life, and is informative and fun to converse with between lives.

Telly intrigues me with stories of his other lifetimes. He likes to live out colorful lives and says he has no time for dull, uninteresting lives.

THE GODDESS ISIS

Isis is another channel-board friend. Isis is the female energy. The Goddess Energy. Isis has always existed, has always been - because there is no beginning and no end.

Conversing with The Goddess, on the channel board, has become one of my favorite pastimes.

Isis has said that, as a collective population, we haven't been very aware of the Female energy during the latter centuries. We have, in fact, welcomed a predominantly Male energy into our lives and blocked out the Female.

The Female population allowed the Male energy to take their power. Allowed, because energy cannot be taken away, it can only be given away.

We lost our balance of energy. We lost the yin and yang from our lives.

This resulted in the scales of life tipping to one side in favor of all that is masculine.

In a world devoid of the Atlantean and Lemurian influences of femininity, Male dominance emerged.

Males became the figureheads in the church and all other places of power.

Females allowed themselves to become the "lesser than".

Sadly, too, the native races "felt" the wave of change and, to a lesser extent, followed a similar pattern.

As a result, the God Source, the All That Is, was now no longer referred to as God/Goddess/All That Is.

All references to the Female were outlawed.

The singular Male name of God was issued by the Males.

We now conveniently had a Male God. And, strangely enough, the heads of the church dictated that God had now become a God of judgment.

Ludicrous as it sounds, we believed pure love was now judging us. Not only judging, but condemning us to hell and damnation if we went against the rules and regulations of our now Male-dominated society.

Imbalance became the order of the day.

Male children became all-important to the human race. The eldest son held the favored position in a family.

He was "entitled" to inherit, he was "entitled" to rule.

And rule he did.

The male now ruled the family, he ruled the money, the places of education, the courts of the land and, of course, the vote.

The Female energy, the Goddess energy still existed. It didn't go away. We just didn't allow it to come through.

We do need the wonderful Male energy, however. Without it there would also be an imbalance of the yin and yang.

One is just as important as the other.

Many of us living on the Earth today have chosen to come back at this particular time, to be a part of the re-emergence of the Goddess energy.

Not in a hostile, overpowering way, for the Goddess would never be hostile or overpowering.

But to bring again to our planet the full Female energy. The Goddess energy.

On April 24, 1994 (April 23 in the Northern Hemisphere), our planet Earth linked with the star Sirius.

On this day the vortex of Sirius opened and the Goddess energy - that softer energy - emerged. The vortex will keep on reopening on the same day each month, leading up to and beyond the turn of the century.

With this, we immediately experience the results of a much needed softening of our hearts and beliefs.

We saw a wise black leader become the President of South Africa, followed up with a peace treaty between Israel and Jordan.

Are we watching at this very moment, as I write this book, the wonder of peace in Northern Ireland?

With Earth's linking with Sirius comes an escalation of the manifestation of whatever we are concentrating on at the moment.

Nelson Mandella had been campaigning on equal rights for his country for years and, suddenly, equality arrived.

Isis suggests we concentrate on the solution, not the problem.

Lazaris has spoken, in depth, on the same issues of the vortex of Sirius opening and the re-emergence of the Goddess.

The beautiful name of Isis is written permanently on my channel board. We talk often and, at times, long into the night.

As a very young child, I was aware of the Goddess and the name Isis. To me Isis was an Angel. An Angel to talk to, as I conversed with my "imaginary friends".

When I first learned the alphabet, long before starting school, I felt the emotion of pride swell up in this child and I asked Isis, "Isis can you spell?"

My finger started to move unaided to the letter Y and then slowly to the letter E and then on to S.

Y.E.S. Yes!

A three-letter word that I'd already learned, along with CAT and DOG.

Isis and I now had a secret.

Isis could spell!

And so could Uncle Harry.

UNCLE HARRY VISITS

I first met Uncle Harry in Grandfather's old house, at Walang in the central west of New South Wales. His photograph hung on the wall, along with other family members who had left this life long ago.

One evening, after I had been put to bed, I lay listening to the drone of adult voices. The faint sounds of conversation floated up the hallway.

Uncle Harry appeared from out of nowhere and sat on the end of my big brass bed.

"Good day Dawn," he smiled. "Or should I say good evening?"

"Hello Uncle Harry. I know who you are. Your photo is on the wall. You are my Great-Great-Uncle Harry."

And so the friendship began.

Uncle Harry and I had many long conversations about his horses. He had loved them so much. Uncle Harry also loved to dance and to laugh.

"If you can't laugh, Dawn, always smile. Promise me you will always smile."

"I will, Uncle Harry, I will."

The family members were shocked, beyond belief, to learn of Uncle Harry's visits. I couldn't understand what all the fuss was about.

Apparently he had died many years before. He didn't look dead to me! "And what if he was? So what?" were the thoughts of this small child. "Doesn't make any difference to me."

I soon learned not to talk about him. Instead of being put to bed early, I was now allowed to stay up until I fell asleep.

That way they could "keep an eye on me".

I was allowed to amuse myself with the alphabet. I was also allowed - encouraged - to put words together.

And I did!

Conversations with Uncle Harry flourished. My knowledge of the family history did also. I even knew the measurements of the old Shirlaw property where Grandfather had lived all his life. I knew that the family had settled there in 1841.

I also knew the family's secrets.

My spelling ability amazed one and all. And in a family where you were expected to spell beyond your years anyway, this was an amazing event.

Uncle Harry had also excelled at spelling!

CHAPTER SEVEN

PAST LIVES I

The Big White House on the Corner .... *Page 108*

I'm a Little Dutch Girl .... *Page 114*

A Past Life with Seth .... *Page 117*

I'm on My Way to Kill the King .... *Page 119*

From Riches to Rags .... *Page 122*

A Black Man in Africa .... *Page 127*

The Theaters of Life .... *Page 130*

King Charles' Mistress .... *Page 132*

Telepathy in the Future .... *Page 132*

Feeding Christians to the Lions .... *Page 136*

> *There is only one Race...*
> *the Human Race.*
> - **Joseph McClenton**

I tend to think of life as a stage play, in which we each have a role. The story can sometimes seem stressful and boring; it really helps to take a break and go home between acts.

This can be done simply, by meditating. Meditation puts us in touch with our soul - with who we really are. I liken it to "going home".

Some of us don't go home for decades. We stay at the theater and concentrate entirely on the play. We mix only with the actors who are in our play. We forget who we really are.

We forget that first of all we are a soul. A soul who happens to be playing a brief role in a drama called "The Physical Life".

We actually come to believe the play is real.

In these stage plays of life, we choose the role we wish to experience and the location of where this lifetime will played out.

We write the script, and produce and direct the whole drama.

We alone cast the other players or make agreements as to who will play which role. Sometimes we agree to play a part for a short while only.

If we're not careful, we can easily forget that it is only a play, an illusion. Instead, we start to believe, more and more, that life is real.

There are no rules about "sticking to the script". We are the ones who make the rules.

We are free to make change. We are not held by binding contracts.

The role of life is meant to be fun. We only come back here to have fun. There are no strings attached. Fun is the real reason we are here.

It can be fun to alter the script and turn a sad play into a successful comedy or maybe a happy love story.

Most of us will mourn a player who leaves our production to have a break between roles, or to take on another role in another play in life.

We just don't think of celebrating the life (or role) they have played. Where are the celebrations and the thanks for the time they have spent in our play?

Why don't we accept their right to call an end to their role?

Instead we pretend they had no choice in their leaving. That there is no way they would have left our chosen role for them of their own accord.

Instead of celebrating their choice to move on to possibly bigger and better things, we choose to mourn their exit - their transition.

I think we call this death!

As a clinical hypnotherapist, I often have the pleasure of regressing people to their past lives.

Sometimes they also wish to experience their future lives.

As a small child I often had flashes of other lifetimes.

THE BIG WHITE HOUSE ON THE CORNER

When I watched my mother prepare a meal or attend to the home I would often say to her, "If we still lived in the big white house on the corner, the one with all the servants, you wouldn't have to make our dinner. Cook would do it for you."

Mother would shake her head in bewilderment at this strange child she had brought into the world, and give her usual reply. "We have never lived in a big white house on a corner, never!"

I couldn't understand how she could forget so easily.

I now know that the memory was from another lifetime.

One day during a past-life session, I was thrilled to find myself in that particular lifetime. And overjoyed to find my "Big white house on a corner."

It was the early 1930's and I worked as a successful actress in the movie industry.

My mother from this life was my secretary and business manager, and "lived in" at the same house.

For a while I felt as if I had really "come home".

I could actually smell the fragrant flowering shrubs in the huge surrounding gardens. I marveled at the masses of color. Reds, yellows, golds, apricots, and pinks of every shade filled this exquisite garden.

Instinctively I looked to where I knew my familiar herb garden would be - and there it was!

Did the planting of this garden really take place, so long ago? A whole lifetime ago?

It was as if time had stood still. I was overcome with emotion and began to sob. "It seems as if it were only yesterday," I cried.

I called to my animals and laughed as they came running. One reindeer, two Dalmatians, a Great Dane, and an assortment of cats, all wanting to be fondled and fussed over at once.

When the greetings were over, they all bounded off to enjoy the grounds of their home - "the big white house on the corner".

A man looked after the garden for me, a man named Harvey. I knew he loved the animals dearly. I was also aware that Harvey trained the dogs and took great care of them.

It seemed as if I had never been away and yet I was fully aware of my present life. Aware, also, that I was connecting with the "past".

I seemed to be observing and participating at the same time.

It was during another session that I suddenly had an overwhelming desire to go again to that lifetime - this time to experience the childhood part. During my previous visit I'd been an adult.

All I have to do is ask.

I looked down at my feet and noticed that I was wearing small shoes, stockings and a long red-and-white check skirt. On top of this was a frilled apron with a pocket.

I stood outside what looked to be a redwood house, with a very steep roof.

A heavy-set, middle-aged woman with golden hair sat watching me from the verandah. I was aware that she looked after me and yet I knew she wasn't my mother.

I wasn't aware of having a mother at all.

I exchanged smiles with a man who was busy tending the garden.

My father from this life!

There he was, as large as life, smiling at me and growing his beloved flowers. He didn't look the same. His build was heavier and his face much rounder and yet I knew, beyond doubt, that this was the same person.

My heart skipped a beat as I felt the love well up inside, that very special love, reserved only for fathers and daughters.

I had the same father in both lifetimes.

As I looked at the Canadian redwood house with the steep sloping roof, I gasped at the familiar panoramic beauty of the snow-topped mountains in the background. They were breathtaking.

I again felt the emotions one equates with returning home.

It was as if I had been away for a very long time, from the place I truly loved, and now I was experiencing all the emotions of returning.

I realized I was familiar with the interior of the house even though I stood outside in the yard during this visit.

Familiar with the furniture, the floor rugs, the

bed quilts and even the blue-and-white dishes on the shelves in the kitchen.

Since going back into that life, I have had the burning desire to collect blue-and-white china dishes. At the last count the tally is four such dinner sets. A visit into another lifetime resulted in a shopping spree in the china shops of Sydney.

Work and home were my main focus in that life. I'm not aware of any relationship or marriage at all.

As I left that life and looked back at my physical body, I felt detached from it. Almost the way one discards a garment that is no longer needed.

I had no regrets or worries about the future of my animals at all. I had left the home and all of my possessions to Harvey.

This "death" occurred on a sound stage in Hollywood, not long before my thirtieth birthday. Not a long life, but a happy and successful one.

Is this then the reason I feel completely at home in Los Angeles?

I'M A LITTLE DUTCH GIRL

I've had flashes of many other lifetimes, too. It happens frequently.

When I was a child, I frequently "saw" a young Dutch girl who actually danced in the traditional Dutch clogs. She sometimes appeared in my dreams.

As a child I had many flashes of her, without realizing that I was watching myself.

Going back into past lives put an end to the mystery.

I was under a light state of hypnosis to experience past lives, and enjoying the trip through the time tunnel.

Suddenly I felt the urge to stop the journey and step outside of my tunnel.

As I did so, I realized I was a child in Holland. A cool breeze swept around me, and the memory of my favorite jacket stirred. My beautiful new jacket, the one my grandmother had made for my birthday, my eighth birthday.

I was aware that it was only a few days since that birthday, but where was my jacket?

I was in trouble for losing it and it just had to be found before dark.

The whole family had called me a "careless and undeserving" child. Low self-esteem crept in and I agreed fully with them.

I was careless and I deserved to be punished. I really loved that jacket and I was so happy when Grandmother presented it to me. Now it was gone. All gone!

"I want my jacket back, I just want my jacket back," I cried as I walked through the long grass.

A brightly colored butterfly appeared and I followed it. The butterfly darted backwards and forwards, and suddenly flew high into the air and over a rise as if to say "Follow me".

I knew the butterfly had come to help me and so I followed it.

I followed it until it alighted on a small mound, to wait for me to catch up.

When I did catch up, the butterfly flew high and hovered for a moment, before sweeping down and landing right on my jacket.

The beautiful, magical butterfly had led me to the exact place where I had left it. I was the happiest girl in the world as I skipped home to tell the family the good news.

Dancing was my love in this lifetime in Holland. My dancing clogs and new jacket were all I desired.

Childhood was wonderful. But as I grew up, the excitement of that life somehow diminished. Life had become structured and repetitious now that childhood had ended.

The years went by and I lived to a ripe old age. As I left that lifetime I thought "Hmm! That was pleasant but also a little boring".

I decided that maybe I should have left just before becoming an adult.

I stopped to look at my peaceful old lifeless body, and thought, "I really do need a new one, it's time for a change of body and a whole new life."

A PAST LIFE WITH SETH

I once shared a life with Seth.

Yes! The entity Seth, the energy essence personality.

This was another Canadian lifetime. A life as a male saloon keeper!

My saloon had an overly long bar and was the favorite haunt of the local lumberjacks.

Seth and John, a famous Australian actor who lived in Sydney in this present life, and is now my channel board guide, were my friends and drinking partners.

As I found myself in this past life, I recognized someone from my present existence. Max, my brother, was one of the rowdy group of lumberjacks drinking down at the far end of the bar.

He wasn't a relative. Max was one of my favorite "regulars".

He had bright red hair and a raucous laugh. The soul does recognize a familiar soul, regardless of the body it is residing in. It just seems to be aware instantly of those we know and love.

I recognized one of Max's lumberjack friends also: his own son from this present life.

Describing that environment and the people to my husband, who was regressing me and recording the session, I said, "We certainly do reincarnate in groups. I throw him (referring to Max) out of the saloon quite often, but he never seems to hold a grudge."

When I visited Canada in this present lifetime, I wanted to kiss the ground the moment I stepped off the aircraft.

I had no idea at the time why I was so overwhelmed to be on Canadian soil. I'm usually "cool, calm and collected". I was in a state of excitement and joy, and I guess the most restless person who ever lined up in the Customs queue.

When a friendly official took me aside, gave me a cup of coffee and asked me all about my visit, it didn't occur to me that he might be suspicious of this highly excited person.

I now know that subconsciously I would have been aware of my other lifetimes, including the happy Canadian ones, when I "first" landed there.

So sorry, Mister Customs Officer! I promise to contain my excitement next time, now I know why Canada means so much to me.

I'M ON MY WAY TO KILL THE KING

Paul and I were both reared in meat-eating families and yet we never felt happy about taking a life just to have a meal. It seemed such an unnecessary waste of life.

The day came when we gave it all away.

Some years ago we were having dinner with our friends, Margaret and Eddie. Margaret mentioned her vegetarian girlfriend's philosophy of "How can I eat animals when I love them so much?" A girl who shared my compassion for the animals of the world.

"If she can do it, I can!" I said. And I did! In fact, we both did. We certainly don't believe it is "wrong" to eat animals. Animals eat other animals.

I would suggest, we "prefer" to consume brown rice and lentils as a protein source rather than take the life of a fish, or a chicken or a cow. A purely personal preference!

For many years now, our diet has consisted of brown rice, lentils, vegetables, fruits and salads. Plus all the unhealthy things that most vegetarians don't touch, such as chocolate, wine, cheesecake, and the like.

Given this, we all thought that Paul couldn't kill a thing.

That is until he "went back" to a certain past life.

A famous forensic palmist and hypnotherapist had finished regressing Paul to another lifetime. As I watched the two men emerge from the consulting rooms, I noticed how "white" my husband looked. He looked as if he had "seen a ghost"! He assured me that he was fine and said "I'll tell you about it later."

The session went as follows.

"What are you doing? Tell me all about it."

"I'm in the woods. I'm tramping through the woods."

"Where are you going?"

"I'm going to kill the King. I am on my way to kill the King."

"Oh, gosh! Maybe we should go forward a few days. Yes! Let's go forward a few days and see what's happening. It is now three days later. Can you tell me what you are doing now?"

"Of course I can. I'm tramping through the woods again. I'm returning home."

"Did you kill the King?"

"Yes! I killed the King, of course I killed the King."

"But why? Why did you do such a thing?"

"I was elected by the people to kill him. I was the one chosen to do the job."

"How do you feel about this now that it's happened. I suppose you feel guilty? Do you?"

"No! Of course not! Why would I feel guilty? He had to be killed and somebody had to do it. I just happened to be the one elected to do it."

Maybe this is the reason Paul values all life so highly in this lifetime.

FROM RICHES TO RAGS

Sometimes we can allow our other lifetimes to make impact on this life without being aware of it. We tend to dump fate and karma on ourselves.

I have a friend who works in sales. He is an extremely efficient worker and follows orders to the letter.

However, he is always content to have others make the decisions in life and doesn't like the responsibility of deciding, even on small issues.

He hands over an unopened pay envelope to his wife, who is then responsible for paying the mortgage, looking after the money, and so on. She even lays out his clothing each morning, to save him the decision on "what to wear".

Putting him back to past lives explained a lot.

We first went to a luxurious palace in India. He was so excited to view this life again, this life as a wealthy sultan. A wealthy sultan consumed entirely by his love of his possessions.

He evidently was giving me a tour of his palace, complete with a running commentary on all his favorite solid-gold statues.

I could almost see the colors in the ceilings, the walls and even the floor rugs as he described them in full detail. To hear the excitement in his voice, and to watch him experience the emotions as he relived this lifetime was something I'll never forget.

In the streets just outside the palace, however, people were dying from starvation.

"I avoid going into the streets at all costs," he remembered. "The sight of beggars and deformed people is too disturbing. I hate smelly, ragged people. It's no fun to leave the palace any more."

"Don't you help them?" I asked. "Surely you do something to help?"

I listened in disbelief as he recalled ignoring their plight.

He let them starve to death.

So vast was his wealth that he could have provided for all of them and not even noticed the difference.

We went further forward to where he left that lifetime.

"I am going to reincarnate in India," he said.

"Well let's go to that life, let us find that life where you come back again to India. Search through now, take your time, there's no need to hurry. When you find it, gently raise your right index finger or speak to me. Remember, though, to speak in English and to speak loudly and clearly."

He started to speak again. His voice had altered. He sounded so young!

"I am very ill, very ill," he coughed.

"Are your parents with you? Is someone helping you?" I asked.

"There is no-one who can help. Nobody at all."

"Where are you? Aren't you at home?"

"The streets are my home. I live in the streets. I beg, that is my life. I am a beggar and I have always been a beggar."

"Don't you ever get off the streets? Doesn't your life get better?"

"No, no. I never seem to leave here. There is nowhere else to go."

I brought him further forward, to where he left that life. He described how relieved he felt to be rid of that diseased body, dying as a young child on the streets of India.

"Why did this wretched life take place? Did you have to come back to it?"

"No. There is no such thing as being made to live out a certain life. I chose the experience myself.

"Not to punish myself, but just to have a few short years experiencing a life as a beggar. I thought it may help my growth. I'd lived hundreds of different lives, in many different cultures, but never as a beggar."

I asked him to tell me about the benefits he had received from the experience. He took quite a while to answer.

I waited in anticipation, expecting a long list of all the beneficial results that must have taken place in his spiritual development.

Finally he spoke. "I learned how to beg. I mean, really beg. That's all I learned from being a beggar.

"I would have accomplished more by maybe reincarnating as a person who helps a country to overcome social issues and poverty. That would have been heaps more fun and it would have achieved a lot more."

He was suddenly quiet. Following a session of their past lives, most people are anxious to talk continuously about the experience. They seem to want to go into the detail of their lives in full.

Not so with my friend!

"You are very quiet," I remarked.

"I think I've given my power away in this present life. I seem to have been irresponsible in some lives past and I think I've opted out on the decision-making this time around. Apparently I don't trust myself to be responsible enough yet."

"Maybe you could really concentrate on allowing yourself to make a few small decisions in life. Small ones that won't have an earth-shattering impact. Take baby steps and try to make it a fun project."

He agreed wholeheartedly. He's now going ahead in leaps and bounds - enjoying the outcome of projects he has now taken responsibility for.

Here on the Earth plane we are experiencing Linear time - that is past, present and future - when, in fact, all time is simultaneous.

It is all happening at the same time.

Sometimes that can be a little hard to understand. One day I had the opportunity to see it in action.

A BLACK MAN IN AFRICA

I had been regressed to a life in Africa. I was a young male adolescent with long, thin black legs. I was fascinated by the length of my legs, as well as my skin color.

"Nowadays I have to buy black pantyhose to achieve the same effect," I told my hypnotherapist.

This was a happy fulfilling lifetime. My family lived in a hut in a small village.

Food was plentiful and our scant possessions were all we needed. There was nothing else.

Africa looked a lot like Australia, dry brown earth, green trees and shrubs, clear blue sky, and never-ending space.

I could feel the sun beating down on me and, under hypnosis, I was aware of becoming quite warm.

Our only worry seemed to be the crocodiles in and around the river. We treated them with the greatest respect.

The day I let my attention wander was the day I left that life.

I sat down on the bank of the river and looked carefully around, my keen eyes scanning the water and the surrounding banks for any sign of movement.

Slowly I let my feet, and then my legs, sink into the coolness of the muddy waters.

I knew no more! There must have been an instant when I felt shock and pain, but I wasn't aware of any sensation at all.

I rose up out of my body and watched as I was thrashed backwards and forwards a few times by the huge predator.

I floated further up and looked out over the village. I knew that I was leaving it forever.

I looked back to see the crocodile stashing my body in a small cave under the water. The horrific news had reached the village already.

I watched my family calling out to each other. They seemed to be running around in circles.

Although I heard their wails of anguish and witnessed their grief, it didn't worry me. I seemed to be just an observer.

It was like watching the finale of a drama in action. My only reaction was "Oh well! It's my fault I was taken."

I floated higher up and looked back again.

The ground was now like a huge green field littered with hundreds of stage productions, all playing at once.

I realized I was "starring" in each play. And all at the same time!

They were all happening at the same time.

THE THEATERS OF LIFE

A priest stood watching some Spanish dancers. They were performing in a courtyard adjoining a church. I knew this was Spain. I also knew that I was the priest.

In another area, a group of Greek peasant men also danced, celebrating the birth of a child.

I felt the joy of the new father and just knew that, in fact, I was him. We danced with our arms linked, the pace of the music becoming faster and faster.

I was highly amused to find myself appreciating my own good looks.

I was a preschooler, riding a carousel in France. I fed the Christians to the lions in Rome. I was a housewife in Scandinavia, bent on scrubbing the house from ceiling to floor until it shone.

A planner of festivities in Egypt in partnership with Margaret, a girlfriend from this life.

A pirate on a sailing ship, on lookout for another ship to plunder. A very unhappy boarding-school boy, who only came home to the family at Christmas time.

A convicted male prisoner in medieval England, and a white witch in Scotland.

Working with crystals in Atlantis and loving every moment of it. Spending many years on a spaceship without being on land and hating it.

Lives of many cultures, with skins of many colors. And all of them mine!

No wonder I no longer take life seriously! If I do any project now, it is only on the basis of "How much fun is involved?"

KING CHARLES' MISTRESS

A neighbor of ours, in this life, enjoyed a short relationship with a truck driver after the break-up of her marriage.

I was amazed to find that she was King Charles' mistress and the mother of three of his children in a previous life.

When she described her children as "illegitimate", I reminded her that there is no such thing as an illegitimate child nowadays (certainly not in Australia, anyway).

"I am in England," she reminded me. "My children are illegitimate, why do you say they are not?"

I stood corrected!

Her truck driver had been King Charles. A monarch in one life, a truckie in another.

TELEPATHY IN THE FUTURE

I had just regressed a fellow hypnotherapist to a few past lives. She had described each lifetime in great detail.

The vivid descriptions of the clothing, the heady perfume from the gardens, even the voices of the children in the background - she must have felt the need to fill me in on almost everything that was happening in her lives.

"Do you want to go into the future?" I asked.

"Yes please! Can you really put me into a future life?"

"Of course! But let's see if you have one first."

Kathy found herself a few centuries ahead of our time. She seemed hesitant to talk to me. I asked her to tell me where she was, to give me some information regarding this life she'd found.

She shook her head at me as if to say "No". I watched her smile to herself a few times before a worried look took over.

Still she would not talk! I was receiving facial expressions and nothing else.

Previously she had talked non-stop and now I couldn't get her to start.

I realized I was actually coaching her to give information. The advanced civilization was of great interest to me and I wondered why she wanted to keep it all to herself.

The session was being taped for her, for goodness sake!

I resorted to the Authoritarian style of hypnosis.

"Kathy, I want you to talk to me now. I want you to tell me about the life you are in."

The face showed instant displeasure.

She drew herself up to sit tall and shook her head in annoyance.

"I cannot believe this! I find your methods of communication degrading and unwarranted," she said.

"Please don't bother me again. I am not going to drain my energy by having to converse. Why aren't you using telepathy?"

"Telepathy! Really! No wonder you don't wish to speak. I apologize for intruding. We can talk after our session is over.

"Please take notice of the environment, the occupations and careers, the living conditions, transport and anything else of special interest in this telepathic life of yours.

"Oh! And please retain the memory of everything you experience. I'm taping this for you."

It was only after coming out of hypnosis that Kathy was able to fill me in on her future life. Apparently, the act of talking was draining to her, both physically and emotionally.

When Kathy finally came out of trance, we played back her tape and laughed at her intolerance about speech.

She informed me her future world was devoid of all pollution and overpopulation.

People no longer found it necessary to seek fulfillment through parenthood, she added. The powers that be were campaigning to educate adults on the advantages of producing children and were about to give special status to any producers of the young.

I realized I was hanging onto every word she said.

War and poverty were now only part of recorded history, she explained, and famine or food shortages just didn't exist.

"What a wonderful world!" I exclaimed. "I just might spend a lifetime there also. I'll think about it. It's certainly very tempting."

What a wonderful world to bring children into - and yet the population as a whole no longer desired them.

Parenthood, it seemed, was out of fashion!

"Kathy, maybe I could come back as "Earth Mother" to that same life. You know, surrounded by a large family of children. That should put me in favor with the politicians of this future world. What do you think?"

I thought about my own childhood. The memories flooded back.

FEEDING CHRISTIANS TO THE LIONS

When I was a child I was never allowed to answer back, or be cheeky in any way. I certainly would never have dared.

I did, however, have my own opinions about everything.

Adults, I discovered, could not read my mind!

Whenever I was asked to read from the Bible, or even to hear the story of the feeding of the Christians to the lions, I would think to myself, "All Christians should be fed to the lions!"

What made me have these thoughts? These aren't the thoughts that a "well-brought-up" little girl should have.

Just where did these beliefs come from?

I now know that they came from a past life.

I had just been regressed and was aware that I was in Rome. I wore the traditional uniform of the Roman soldier.

Again, I had come back as a male.

The huge size of the body I was in amazed me. My thick legs were muscled and covered in hair.

My uniform was made of thick brown leather - heavy and uncomfortable.

I was not a pretty sight!

The Gladiators had just left the ring and the spectators were screaming for the lions to appear. Feeding the lions was evidently the main attraction!

The bars were moved back and out strode the lions. They were not in a hurry at all - they were really taking their time.

"Too well fed," I remarked.

With the help of another soldier, I pushed a few men into the ring. It seemed perfectly normal to feed the lions in this manner.

The crowd roared their approval.

Out came a few more of the big cats and in went a few more Christians.

I fed the Christians to the lions!

Hmm! I had also kept the best one for last.

I called to my favorite lion. "Semm, Semm, come Semm!"

Semm came slowly out of an enormous pipe and looked down at me.

He was the largest of the lions.

Truly the King of Beasts.

We made eye contact and I realized that a special bond existed between us. A bond of love! Semm and I actually loved one another!

"I know this lion from somewhere else," I puzzled.

The great eyes widened. I seemed to be drawn into their depths.

I found myself looking into the eyes of Sam. Sam, my Siamese cat, one of the great loves of my life. My lovable Aries feline, with the heart of a lion!

We had often joked that Sam must have been a koala in another lifetime. He always insisted on being carried like a koala, putting both front paws around my neck and cuddling in.

Now I knew that Sam had been a lion, my favorite lion, during a lifetime in Rome.

I fed the "best" Christian to my lion.

"I seem to reincarnate frequently, with my favorite animals and people," I thought as I recalled Sam's funeral service and the wake held for him when he left this life.

Sam went with a little help from the vet, at the end of seventeen-and-a-half memorable years with us.

He truly did have a 'real' wake.

I placed an advertisement in the funeral notice column of the leading national Saturday paper.

In the ad I referred to Sam as our beloved Siamese cat who had departed from this life, and mentioned that all friends who knew and loved Sam were invited to attend his service and wake.

This resulted in a packed house!

I'd felt the urge to let Sam know he was very

special to us. It was great to know, too, that no-one in the whole of Australia, objected to Sam's funeral notice.

CHAPTER EIGHT

PAST LIVES II

My Son the Viking . . . . *Page 145*

The Handicapped Seamstress . . . . *Page 147*

The Food Addict and the Holocaust . . . . *Page 149*

The French Riding Instructor . . . . *Page 154*

A White Child . . . . *Page 157*

The Dream link . . . . *Page 158*

A Wolf in the Animal Kingdom . . . . *Page 160*

Fear of Dogs - Love of Cats . . . . *Page 163*

A Life as a Meerkat . . . . *Page 168*

My Daughter - My Headmistress . . . . . . *Page 169*

MY SON THE VIKING

*M*y realization that we tend to reincarnate in groups was reaffirmed when I found myself in yet another lifetime.

I realized that I was sitting in a small sailing craft. Fog surrounded us. It was so heavy it was almost impossible to see through it.

A man stood at the front of the boat, blowing a huge horn. A Viking's horn. I listened to its lonely sound as it rang out into the miserable morning.

I knew that this man was my brother. I also knew he was in charge of the voyage home.

I was aware that I was a young female, wearing clothing fashioned from the hides of animals. Designer wear did not exist in that life!

The hides smelled as if the tanning method could do with some improvement.

I wasn't very enthusiastic at all about the journey I was undertaking. Water sloshed around in the bottom of the boat and I was aware of the intense cold.

The smell of the salt water hung in the foggy air.

My wisdom tooth ached and I was cold and hungry.

The fog eventually started to clear and I was now able to see the features of my companions.

My brother, the Viking who had been blowing the horn, turned around and I was startled to recognize him from my present life. My brother in another life, my son Sonny, from this life.

Sonny still looks like a Viking. You could place a set of horns on his head and we would have, to all appearances, a ready-made Viking! Maybe it's his hair.

I wonder what he will say when he reads this book! He could write a book on his present life. Maybe he will one day.

THE HANDICAPPED SEAMSTRESS

My next-door neighbor had often mentioned that past lives fascinated her. One day I said "Why don't we find out just how fascinating your own past lives are?"

In this life Samantha is a psychiatric nurse.

Her happiest past life astounded me.

"I can't walk at all," she said. "I have no control over my legs. My family are so good to me though, they carry me anywhere I need to go."

"Don't you have a wheelchair?" I asked.

"Of course not! What a silly thing to say. I sit and sew all day long. There's no need for a wheelchair."

Samantha went on to describe her needlework. The intricate patterns, the fine stitches. She described the tablecloth that took a year to make, even though she spent every day working on it.

She spoke of the plans she had for future sewing projects. She felt the need to press on with her work and to put all her effort into making each perfect piece.

"Sewing certainly appears to be your specialty in this life," I observed.

"Yes! I know. I would never think of doing anything else. Creative pursuits such as painting, for instance, would never interest me.

"I just want to be left alone to sew. That is all I ask, just leave me alone and allow me to get on with the job!"

I "smelled a rat"!

"How long is this life?" I asked.

"A very long life. I'm an old, old lady when I pass on."

"Do you sew right up until the end?" I asked, thinking I probably knew the answer.

"Until the day I stopped breathing," she sighed.

We then went forward, to where she had just "stopped breathing". I asked if she knew the reason for her handicap in that life.

"I chose to be handicapped. I wanted a life devoted to sewing and this was the perfect way to achieve it.

"As a handicapped person, I was free to put all my effort into my work, without any excuses. I had no other responsibilities at all."

This was quite an eye-opener. Samantha had deliberately chosen to be confined. This had allowed her the opportunity to sit and sew, without interruption or criticism from others.

"The things we do!" I joked after she came out of trance.

THE FOOD ADDICT
AND THE HOLOCAUST

As a clinical hypnotherapist, I take people for hypnosis for other reasons apart from past lives.

On some occasions I have applied hypnosis and suggested that my client "go back to the cause of the problem, to where the trouble first started" - thinking, of course, of their younger days.

Imagine my surprise to find them in a past life. Not only in a past life, but also "to where the problem first started".

And this has happened with folk who, until now, have not even believed in past lives.

One such person is a dear friend, Kate.

Kate had an addiction to food and, as a true food addict, would never admit to overeating.

At times she would unwittingly mention the three delicious hamburgers she'd eaten for lunch. Three tiny ones of course! Or the succulent dinner cooked in butter and cream, that she planned for the evening meal.

Her intake of fat was every doctor's nightmare.

Kate constantly complained about her weight and had a habit of saying, "I shouldn't be overweight. I hardly eat anything at all, I just can't understand it."

I would laugh and say, "Look, when you finally want to stop indulging, and really want help, I'll be there for you."

Kate, at thirty years of age, could not sit on a sofa. She was unable to raise herself from low, soft seating and started to choose a higher chair with a hard seat.

Chairs with arms were out, of course, as she could no longer fit into them.

The day finally came when Kate really wanted help.

It was possibly the quickest and easiest end to overeating I have ever witnessed.

The entire cure took one single one-hour session.

We were both amazed and delighted.

When I knew she was in trance, I uttered the magic words, "Go back now to the cause of the problem. To the time the problem first started.

"When you've found this time I want you to let me know. Just tell me that you are there."

Kate spoke very softly. "I am now where the problem started.

"I am so hungry and so frightened and I mustn't cry. If I cry someone will hear me."

"Kate tell me why you are hungry."

"Because I have to wait until it is safe for them to bring me food. I am hiding in the wall and some days I don't get any food at all."

The hairs on the back of my neck stood up. I felt a little uneasy.

"Tell me all about it. Tell me where you are and why you are hiding in the wall."

"I have to hide in the wall or the soldiers will take me away, like they took Mama and Ruthie."

I could hardly believe my ears. Kate who did not believe in past lives was evidently in one at this moment.

"Who are the soldiers?"

"They are Hitler's men. They are looking for any Jews and I must be quiet. My stomach hurts so much, it's hard not to cry."

I was almost in tears myself.

"How long is it since you have eaten?"

"Not yesterday, I think it was the day before that, but I'm not sure."

"Kate I asked you to go back to where your problem with overeating first started. Are we in the right place?"

Yes! We were in the right place - "the time the problem first started".

No-one was more surprised than Kate. She had never expected to find the source of her problem in another lifetime.

Before this session, she had believed we live one lifetime only. The knowledge that she had starved to death during another life, had an amazing effect on her.

We talked at length about her past life. The holocaust had always meant "something" to her, she admitted. She had read every piece of information available on it. She had often wondered why she had such a compulsion to keep scrapbooks of any information she could collect on the holocaust.

Kate is not Jewish in this life, but has always had enormous compassion and respect for the culture and the people.

Kate's craving for excessive amounts of food vanished from that moment. She had lost all desire to overeat.

No further sessions needed.

It was just so easy!

THE FRENCH RIDING INSTRUCTOR

I often have the pleasure of regressing my Tazmanian friend Evelyn. On one occasion she had come to find out about a specific life. A past life that she already had some knowledge of.

That life had taken place a few centuries ago in France.

Evelyn is a riding instructor and a colleague of high profile equestrian Lisa Joyce.

When Lisa channeled Silzaar for Evelyn, Silzaar mentioned her previous life as a male French riding instructor. Evelyn was astounded.

The teaching methods instilled in her early in this present life were not of her choosing. She believed them to be too harshly disciplined and devoid of love.

A few years ago, Evelyn met an instructor from England who shared her beliefs and his own teaching methods with her. She said it was "like coming home".

The new equitation seemed so familiar to her. As if she had known it and maybe even used it before.

Silzaar advised Evelyn that she certainly had used the same methods in another lifetime. Not only had she used them, she had actually written books about the subject.

He gave her the name of the book and the name of the author. Her own name from her previous lifetime!

Miracles do happen!

Evelyn sought out and found an autobiography of herself from this other lifetime. An incredible achievement.

Thank you Silzaar!

I put Evelyn into trance, in order to find her life as the riding instructor in France.

She described the green of the countryside and the surrounding stables. "I can actually smell the hay and the horses," she said. "I recognize many of the horses, I even remember their names."

"Tell me about your life," I suggested.

"My classical equitation is frowned upon in some circles. Many believe that harsh discipline is the only way to train an animal. My results speak for themselves.

"My horses love to work with me. They are aware that I love them and they love me back. We work together as a team, and I make sure the horses are happy at work. Many methods are outdated and should be abolished."

Evelyn certainly was the riding instructor Silzaar reputed her to be.

When she had experienced enough of that lifetime, I asked Evelyn if she wanted to find another life.

"I would love to," came the definite answer.

A WHITE CHILD

"My name is Caroline and I live in the Deep South," Evelyn affirmed in a little-girl voice.

"The deep south of where?" I asked.

"The deep south of the United States of America."

"Tell me about your life as Caroline," I ventured.

"I am wearing my black patent-leather shoes and a new dress," Caroline said. "We help to save the black people, when they escape."

"Are you a white person?" I asked.

"Yes, I am. And my mother and daddy are too. The other white people don't know that we help the black people.

"My daddy can get them to the North."

Evelyn went on to describe the adventurous life she shared with her family in the Deep South. This was a fulfilling life for her and when the time came to finally say "good bye" to that existence, she sighed and said, "I enjoyed every moment of it!"

THE DREAM LINK

Most dreams are linked to our other lifetimes, to the other aspects of ourselves.

If all time is simultaneous, then our lives are all happening at the same time.

While we sleep, the physical body may rest, but not the "me" that we are.

From my experience, we seem to meet up with our other selves from other lives during the dream state.

A little like a family reunion!

Have you ever dreamed that you were making love to your favorite movie star? It is quite possible that you are linking with a past life where this actually happened.

When you dream of being chased by another person, trying desperately to outrun them in a state of fear and panic, it is highly probable that this scenario did take place. You have probably lived a past life of adventure and intrigue.

Quite often when you meet someone for the first time, there is an immediate emotional reaction towards them.

The emotions of love or hate. Like or dislike.

This reaction doesn't take place with every new meeting, of course! But I'm sure most of us have experienced it at some time or other.

This instant emotional reaction usually comes from a past-life association with the "new" person.

Your unconscious mind, or your subconscious mind, carries all memory of all lives.

No wonder we can find ourselves "prejudging".

A WOLF IN THE ANIMAL KINGDOM

John is a client who often comes for a Reading.

One day, following a consultation, he mentioned that he had recently attended a past-life workshop.

When the hypnotherapist instructed the class to look down at their feet to see if they were wearing shoes, he found himself looking at two hairy paws.

When he mentioned this, his instructor said "Stop fooling around and don't be so silly."

"Not only did I see paws, I could feel them. I knew they were mine," he said. "Do you know what I'm talking about?"

I certainly did!

"Don't be too critical of your hypnotherapist," I suggested. "As with other things, we sometimes have to see these things first and believe them second.

"The truth is that it's the other way around.

"'You'll see it when you believe it', as Dr Wayne Dyer tells us in his best-selling book of the same title."

I told John of my personal experience with past-lives. "I started out in the mineral kingdom. After that I became part of the plant kingdom, then the animal kingdom, followed by the human kingdom.

"I believe it is a transition of sorts and all part of our journey home to The God source. To God/Goddess/All That Is.

"Next time you see me, John, why not have a past-life regression into your animal kingdom?"

And he did!

John went easily into trance.

I suggested he find that same lifetime, where he had paws instead of feet.

I used almost the same method of "looking down" and asked him to see if he could find his paws again.

"I've found them. I've found them," John exclaimed. "I have four paws."

"I hope so," I said. "Tell me about this animal life of yours."

He described the scene around his lair. The ground was covered thickly with snow and the branches of the trees were weighed down with it.

"I am a wolf, I seem to be a female wolf. I'm a mother of cubs. I have three cubs.

"They are almost old enough to venture out. What a good life! I'm really enjoying it.

"I am a great hunter and I bring home plenty of small animals to my cubs. I love to run at lightning speed, not only to catch and kill, but also for the sheer thrill of running fast."

"What color are your cubs?"

"They are somewhere between black and white, like a gray. There is only black and white. I don't see in color at all. I see in detail, I think.

"I know I can spot movement from a mile away.

"The smell of meat is different too. My sense of smell is not the same."

When John came out of trance, he described his regression as astounding. He had always had a deep love of wolves and, as a child, had collected photographs and cut-outs of wolves from magazines.

I told John of the man who loved cats, but loathed dogs. All dogs, large and small.

FEAR OF DOGS - LOVE OF CATS

Mr X had never had close contact with a dog, never a bad experience with one. He just knew he couldn't stand them.

He did, however, enjoy having a regular Reading.

During a recent business consultation with him, I became aware of a small man standing next to him.

Although the small man's appearance was very subtle, I could see that two fingers were missing from his left hand.

He held out his left hand to me and then touched his bow tie repeatedly, as if indicating the importance of it.

By now, my head was receiving a few light taps on the back, just below the crown. I knew that information would follow through, as it always does after the tapping.

The name Alf kept "coming through" then the words, "I got to wear the bow tie after all."

In the middle of a sentence on just how Mr X's business would prevail, I found myself saying, "Alf says to tell you that he got to wear the bow tie after all."

"Alf?"

"Yes Alf. Alf who has left this life and has two fingers missing from his left hand."

"Alf? my Uncle Alf?"

"Was he your uncle? Well, he is here now, wearing a bow tie and he wants you to know that he got to wear the bow tie after all.

"Does that make any sense to you?"

It certainly did!
Mr X had given his Uncle Alf the bow tie for his birthday. Alf died just a few days later.

For his burial, the family had dressed Uncle Alf in his best suit and his new bow tie. He had worn his new tie, if only to his own funeral.

Then Uncle Alf really threw the spanner into the works.

"We were cats together in another life," he said. "That's the reason you're scared of dogs today."

I passed the message on.

Mr X was flabbergasted! He knew, beyond all doubt, that this was his uncle.

This resulted in a past-life regression to find the life they shared as cats together.

He would not be an easy subject. Mr X was intense and nervous.

"Uncle Alf must have been joking, when he said I was a cat," he mused.

Surprisingly, he went deeply into trance. I thought it best for him to find a few human lives before taking him to a feline one.

He found a life as a prizefighter in Ireland, and another one as an early settler in Australia.

This allowed him to be more comfortable with the whole process.

Mr X was a cat all right. A cat forced to live on a roof, to avoid the savage dogs in the yard below. He spent a lifetime keeping out of their way.

I remember smiling as he described his gray and white stripes and his snowy white paws to me. He described Uncle Alf as a large black-and-white tom cat.

They both hated the snarling dogs who restricted their lives. They also had many narrow escapes. "Very hairy" were the words Mr X used to describe some of his near misses with death.

Before bringing him out of hypnosis, we discussed his fear of dogs and the reason behind it.

With my subject's permission, I removed the fear of dogs from his memory.

Weeks later Mr X rang to ask if he could drop by and show off his very own dog.

"What breed is it?" I asked.

"Don't want to tell you, Dawn, I want to surprise you."

He arrived with a white French poodle pup. He had fallen in love with the pup the moment he saw her.

Her named her Chantelle.

We took turns in nursing and cuddling Chantelle. Even my cattle dog loved her. Not that that surprised me. Our Kimbles lives like a French poodle in this life and I suspect she has been one in another life.

Mr X has overcome his dislike of canines. Now, when he meets someone out walking their dog, he stops and asks permission to say hello and to give the dog a pat on the head.

"Knowing why I disliked dogs before has cured me of not liking them now," he told me.

My own experience in regressing to the animal kingdom was an extremely emotional experience.

A LIFE AS A MEERKAT

I found myself as a meerkat in a past life - a little South African mongoose.

A very stressed-out meerkat in a colony of stressed-out meerkats.

Our whole focus was on the act of survival. The survival of the young was every meerkat's responsibility. We took turns at keeping watch for the enemies. I marveled at how organized we were.

These were the circumstances I found myself in, as I stepped out of the time tunnel and into my meerkat life.

I nervously herded a litter of young ones out of the burrows as other meerkats stood on tiptoes to look as far afield as possible. There was no way I would let my guard down, not even for a split second. This was a life which revolved around stress.

I felt relieved to leave that life behind and bask in the harmony between lives.

I have always had a deep affection for meerkats and yet I have only seen them through the media in this lifetime.

MY DAUGHTER - MY HEADMISTRESS

Imagine my surprise when I stepped out of the time tunnel, during yet another past-life regression, to recognize my daughter from this life.

I realized I was a new student at a finishing school. I had traveled from America to attend this exclusive school in Switzerland.

This venture was not of my choosing and the thought of the years ahead, spent in a foreign country, were almost too much to bear.

And now as I waited to meet the headmistress, I found it hard to hold back the tears.

Suddenly the huge doors were opened and out came a smiling, pleasant young woman. She greeted me with a warm welcome and instantly made me feel at ease.

I found myself being treated as an important guest, when I had expected to be confronted by an overbearing old disciplinarian.

She made me feel very special and mentioned that the whole school would officially welcome me in the morning. When I left her study, I felt as if I would never want to leave this school. Never!

I recognized the headmistress from that life as my daughter from this life.

Suellen has always been aware that she was a teacher in previous lives.

Now my headmistress in Switzerland, in the late eighteenth century, is living a life as my daughter in the twentieth century.

Most people are not interested in exploring their plant kingdom life at all.

What a shame!

What stories there would be. It would have made an interesting chapter.

CHAPTER NINE

Confirmations

Luck with the Aquarian . . . . *Page* 173

The Blind Date . . . . *Page* 176

The Perilous Position . . . . *Page* 179

A Home at Surfers Paradise . . . . *Page* 181

The Successful Bankrupt . . . . *Page* 182

Do Not Travel on the Coach . . . . *Page* 184

The Winning Trips . . . . *Page* 186

Manifesting a Dream Home . . . . *Page* 188

Infidelity . . . . *Page* 191

Help for a Psychic . . . . *Page* 193

The Deceptive Clairvoyant . . . . *Page* 195

Visions of a Lost Ring . . . . *Page* 196

A Lost Dog . . . . *Page* 198

The Cat Who Wasn't Lost . . . . *Page* 201

The Wife with Red Hair . . . . *Page* 204

A Change of Husband . . . . *Page* 206

Some of the most exciting and rewarding bonuses to come from readings, are the confirmations that come from clientele.

The phone rings and an excited client will be on the line.

"I just had to tell you," is their opening line. "I had to tell you that your predictions came true."

This was also Ron's opening remark.

LUCK WITH THE AQUARIAN

"Take a few deep breaths, Ron," I coached. "Calm down. You're too excited to speak. Take a deep breath and start again. I can't understand a word you are saying."

"Remember I told you I had to pay twenty-five-thousand dollars by the end of the month and that there was no way in the world I would be able to," Ron stammered.

"I was worried sick about the debt. I was frantic. Do you remember what you said to me, Dawn? Do you?"

"Remind me please Ron, I usually lose the information that comes to me as soon as I pass it on to you."

"You said not to worry about the money, the money would be in my account days before I had to pay it out.

"You said you weren't concerned about my finances at all. I would be able to pay the debt on time. It would be taken care of, you predicted, out of my winnings with the Aquarian.

"Dawn, you mentioned you were more concerned about my health that I'd been neglecting, and that I needed a good checkup.

"All through the Reading you kept telling me that the money would just be taken care of. When I walked out of your door you said it was very important that I call in at my doctor's surgery on the way home.

"The last thing I wanted to do was waste time sitting around a medical center. Sure I'd been feeling terrible, but I associated the pains in the abdomen with the stress caused by my lack of finances.

"The pains were getting worse and I felt like death warmed up."

"Go on!" I invited, sensing his excitement. "Tell me the outcome."

"Well, when Doctor said my appendix needed to be taken out straight away, I told her about you. I told her that you'd said I absolutely must have a checkup on my way home.

"I also told her about the money I owed and how you said the win with the Aquarian would take care of the debt.

"I told her, too, that I didn't know an Aquarian.

"Now here's the amazing part. The doctor said,

'What a shame it's not my star sign. However, my receptionist happens to be an Aquarian."

"Don't tell me, I can see it already," I laughed. "Did you and the receptionist take a ticket together?"

"We did! I gave her my share of the cost and she went out and bought the winning ticket. We won a hundred-thousand dollars, fifty-thousand each."

It was my turn to be delighted. We really had a good laugh about the outcome.

"I'm just so glad I took your advice and went to the doctor," Ron enthused.

No wonder I love my work!

THE BLIND DATE

Jodie is a young friend who lives with us. She was telling us last night about her blind date the previous evening.

Friends of hers, a young married couple, had asked her to dinner. They were matchmaking and had invited a friend to meet the apprehensive Jodie.

When she arrived she was introduced to a man who was in deep conversation with the host.

His conversation encompassed the nudist colonies he attended, and Jodie was not impressed at all.

When the hostess and her mother invited the now indignant Jodie upstairs to view a new purchase, she vented her hostilities on them.

"How could you do this to me," she accused. "He certainly is not anyone I would wish to meet. I would never go to a nudist colony.

"He is too old for me and I suspect he's married. How dare you do this?"

They gasped with amazement then laughed hilariously.

The man she had been introduced to was a neighbor who had called in on his way home - not "Mr Right". Jodie was right about the marriage, the neighbor is very happily married.

The awaited friend arrived. Wayne was well-mannered, well-groomed - and also very apprehensive.

During dinner, he told Jodie that two years ago his clairvoyant had described her to him and said, "You will meet Jodie."

And yes! I turned out to be the same clairvoyant.

Jodie stood on our staircase later, laughing and shaking her head as she filled me in on the previous evening.

I noticed that she was fondling her gold neck chain.

"Oh no! I've lost my gold charm, my golden scissors. It must have fallen off my chain. I couldn't bear to lose it. It's very special to me."

"You will find it. Just look in your bra," I said as I walked away.

Jodie went up to her room and a few minutes later called over the banister, "Dawnie, I found it. It was in my bra."

"I must be psychic!" I laughed.

THE PERILOUS POSITION

A few years ago Jodie took on a government career.

She enjoyed the work, but the distance and traveling left a lot to be desired. The department she worked for was in the mountains, over two hours away.

When recruiting, the government has a habit of advertising, internally, a position that's already filled.

This means that employees from other departments can apply for someone else's job.

The person who holds the position can also apply.

After eleven months in the job, Jodie found herself in this precarious position.

"I don't want to go back to hairdressing," she despaired.

"I predict long life in a government career for you," I told her. "I also see you receiving a promotion."

The interviews for her position took place and a successful applicant was chosen. Jodie, however, was not the one. Her application was unsuccessful.

She was given a week's notice to finish. Someone else had been chosen to take her place.

"I can't understand it," she said. "You are so sure I will stay with the government and yet they tell me I have to finish up on Friday."

Familiar tapping started on the back of my head and the message, "Jodie will not leave the government job," came through.

"You won't be leaving the government job," I repeated. "You are not out of work."

On Wednesday she informed me that her severance money had been paid into her bank account. "I finish on Friday. Two weeks before Christmas and I'm out of work."

"You are not out of work. I know I am not making any sense to you at the moment. You must think I'm out of my tree," I said.

"I just can't see you being out of work. In fact, I predict a wonderful Christmas for you."

The day before she was to finish, Jodie answered the phone at work and found the man who had interviewed her originally, on the line.

"I've just heard the news," he said. "How would you like to come and work for this department?

"You would! Good! Seeing you've already received your holiday pay, why don't you take a week off, enjoy yourself and report to me ready to start on Monday week?"

Monday week was about five days before Christmas. Her new place of work was close to home.

And a Merry Christmas was had by all.

A HOME AT SURFERS PARADISE

Another favorite "show biz" client phoned.

"I just had to let you know that I now have the house you predicted for me, Dawn."

"Tell me about it," I said.

"Well, you said I would own it outright. That it was mine by divine right. You even said 'Surfers Paradise. The house is at Surfers Paradise'."

Alison (not her real name), who was an adopted child, went on to inform me that since seeing me she had found her natural mother.

Mother lived at Surfers Paradise in Queensland.

They had a happy but short-lived reunion.

Mother "passed away" and Alison inherited the house.

The mystery of the house at Surfers Paradise was solved.

THE SUCCESSFUL BANKRUPT

I made another prediction about buying land, to build a new home apparently, to a rather confused client.

The poor girl kept repeating, "But I can't own anything for years. I'm bankrupt. I'm not allowed to own anything yet."

I received an exciting phone call from her about three months later.

"I did go home to New Zealand for Christmas and I had to let you know how amazingly accurate you were," she confirmed.

"All through the Reading you kept saying, 'Don't worry about the fact that you are bankrupt. I see you successfully acquiring land'."

She went on to say, "You even said that, in Capricorn, I will know exactly when I will return to New Zealand to live."

"Tell me the whole story," I suggested.

Her brother, it seems, was quite successful and wanted to help his sister.

He had purchased land at a low price some years ago and it had really grown in value.

His plan was to sell it to her at the price he originally paid. He would draw up an agreement to sell now.

The official sale would take place when her bankruptcy is discharged in two years time. When this happens, she will have enough money saved from her job in Australia to pay for the land without taking out a mortgage.

She will then return to her own country, to a waiting job, and build her dream home.

What a happy ending! I was delighted.

But not so with the call that came in from Western Australia.

DO NOT TRAVEL ON THE COACH

Gloria phoned from Perth, on the other side of this large country.

"Remember when you told me not to travel by coach to Perth?

"Remember you told me I would not enjoy the family Christmas I had planned unless I went by plane?"

I "picked up" the hospital bed as she talked.

"You've had an accident, haven't you Gloria?

But you are out of hospital now, aren't you?"

"You're right! I've spent twelve weeks in hospital and I certainly missed Christmas."

"Gloria, I 'get' deception all around the coach company."

"Right again! They denied that I was on the coach."

I was horrified. Taken to hospital as a result of a coach smash, and the coach company denies she is their passenger?

"I will certainly take notice of you in the future," she said. "I just didn't want to pay the price of the air fare."

My heart went out to Gloria. Spending Christmas in hospital instead of with her family would be very hard to accept.

This was one time an accurate prediction of mine would not bring me happiness. I had predicted that coach travel would bring disaster, and I had suggested to Gloria to alter her plans.

THE WINNING TRIPS

"Good morning Dawn," my neighbor Jonathan called from over the fence.

"Do you remember telling me I had a lucky quick trip away? You said it seemed a little too quick.

"When I asked you where to, you said 'I'm seeing a tropical setting'."

"Go on," I encouraged.

"Well! We had our trip on Wednesday evening."

"What do you mean," I asked, "you had your trip on Wednesday evening?"

"We won an overnight stay at a five-star hotel in Sydney and it included dinner and two tickets to South Pacific."

We had a good laugh over that one.

I also laughed over my daughter's prediction of a trip for me.

Suellen phoned with great excitement in her voice. "You are going to win a trip away and I think it's this week!"

"But I haven't entered any competitions for trips," I said.

"Well you may not have. Somehow you will still win a trip. You will know what I'm talking about by the end of the week."

And I did. I knew exactly what she meant by the end of the week!

I had bought a raffle ticket for a home in Queensland. I was unaware of their 'Early Bird' draw to encourage the early purchase of tickets.

I won the Early Bird draw. Three thousand dollars worth of travel to the destination of my choice.

It was good to be on the receiving end of a prediction for a change.

A couple who really were on the receiving end are two clients, mother and son, who always come for a Reading together.

MANIFESTING A DREAM HOME

When Roberta and Andrew arrive for a Reading, I see Roberta first and then her delightful son.

They are a fun team to read for. Andrew is gay and flaunts the fact. He wants the world to know.

They are best friends as well as being mother and son. I always look forward to seeing them. They are a delight to read for.

They arrived one day to tell me that they had spent the morning looking at exhibition homes. Beautiful homes to be built on your own land.

Andrew had said to his mother "Let's pretend we have all the money we need to buy any house we choose."

Roberta said, "We were like two children, running from room to room, pretending we had just bought the biggest and the best. We really shouldn't be let out!" she laughed.

"Be careful of what you're doing," I cautioned. "You could manifest that actually happening."

"What do you mean?" they chorused together.

"Well what you are doing here is pretending and affirming that the house is yours.

"When you affirm with such desire and joy and enthusiasm, really feeling that you've already received it, you are, in fact, manifesting."

"Manifesting?"

"Yes, manifesting!

"It's a method of consciously creating what you want.

"I used this method when I wanted a closet full of designer clothing, I wore my clothing as if it were designer labeled. I looked after every item as if it had cost a fortune. I washed and pressed each article with the same care I would lavish on designer wear.

"This worked! I now have closets filled with designer labels.

"The method you are using is fun, and fun is another powerful tool to work with. You are experiencing the joy of receiving, prior to receiving.

"I always advise anyone who needs a new car, to wash and polish their old car and drive it as if it were the new one.

"Why not care for your rental flat as if it were your dream home. I'd certainly suggest you keep up the manifesting, I have a very intuitive feeling that you really are creating a home."

They phoned quite often, to give an update on their activities.

I was highly amused to know that they had actually scheduled a permanent Saturday and Sunday visit to "their" exhibition home.

This took priority over all other weekend activities.

"Just be sure you still make it fun," I suggested.

"Don't, at any time, do it out of desperation. Desperation will only result in depression.

"If ever you get to the point where you would rather not visit the home one weekend, then take a break."

My intuition was right.

Andrew and his mother won the amount of money needed to purchase the land of their choice and build the exhibition home they loved so much.

Just the full amount. Nothing over, nothing above and beyond the cost of their dream.

They were thrilled to the depth of their souls. "We were just so lucky!" they repeated over and over.

"Yes!" I agreed. "But only because you created the luck. You both made it happen.

"Be gracious enough to recognize the fact. And do remember to congratulate yourselves on a job well done."

I love happy outcomes!

I couldn't say that about Stephanie's call back, however.

INFIDELITY

Stephanie was a young mother of twins. She had been living with her partner for three years now and the twins were a result of the union.

Unfortunately, her man wasn't happy to find himself a parent. It was no secret that she had deliberately become pregnant, against his wishes.

Love, it seemed, had flown out the window.

He constantly hit out at her and the toddlers. It was an unhappy situation from all sides.

Intuitively, she knew that her partner was involved with other females.

"Women's intuition," she told me. "I have no proof, but somehow I just know.

"I just want proof and then I can leave him with a clear conscience. He hates us and we hate him. I now wish I'd never met him.

"Can you give me that proof?"

Familiar tapping came to the back of my head and I heard myself saying, "I won't need to supply the proof. Your doctor will give you all the proof you need. Try to make an appointment for today."

Later the same day, I received a phone call from Stephanie.

"I have a sexually transmitted disease," she said. "You were right! Doctor gave me all the proof I needed."

This is certainly not my favorite prediction, but both of them will be happier when they live apart from one another.

HELP FOR A PSYCHIC

Among my clientele are many other clairvoyants and psychics. It is quite common to find myself Reading for another Reader.

A high-profile clairvoyant, a very psychic man, had had a robbery at his home. Like many other Readers, he wasn't good at predicting for himself.

Of course, he wanted me to identify the one who robbed him.

It was obvious to the police that the guilty party was familiar with the home.

I closed my eyes and two identical men appeared. I "got" Pisces.

"Who are the twins?" I asked. "I 'get' twin Pisceans and they're males."

"I knew it!" he exclaimed. "I had a feeling that it was those two. I just didn't want to accept it."

"Are they relatives?"

"My nephews. This could cause trouble in the family and I don't want that."

"I am 'getting' a way to avoid that difficulty," I said.

"No-one need know about it. Ask the police to go around to their house with you. Tell your nephews that you won't have them charged, if they return everything now."

I also told him to warn them that he wouldn't be so lenient in the future.

I was delighted to receive a phone call from him. He did have a happy ending!

Apparently when he arrived at his nephews' home accompanied by a police officer, it was to find the twins sitting on his sofa, watching his television set.

Under the circumstances, the brothers were only too happy to cooperate and return their ill-gotten goods.

THE DECEPTIVE CLAIRVOYANT

One morning, as I welcomed my first client for the day, I "felt" that she too was a Reader.

Before I had time to mention it, she made a statement that questioned my intuition.

"I'm not sure I agree with this sort of thing, I'm a shop assistant and I usually don't go to psychics when I need an answer."

It is unlike me not to respond to intuitive flashes. However, on this occasion I did hold back.

We were about five minutes into the Reading when, without warning, our seating arrangements suddenly changed.

One moment I was sitting on a wingback chair, my Reading chair. And now I sat across from it, on a two-seater sofa, looking at my "shop assistant".

We had reversed positions!

For a split second I felt confused. Then the significance of the situation hit me.

"You're a Reader!" I exclaimed. "You are definitely a Reader. We changed places and you were sitting where I sit. That tells me that you, too, are a clairvoyant."

I have only had this happen on two occasions. The sensation is both astounding and enthralling.

VISIONS OF A LOST RING

On some occasions, I admire the ring on a client's finger.

I find myself going into great detail about the setting, the colors and description of the precious stones involved, only to hear them say, "That's amazing! I should have worn that ring today. I'm sorry I left it at home."

It is only then that I realize I'm looking at an empty finger.

There was an occasion when I did the opposite and kept looking at a ring, long after the man told me he'd lost it years before.

"I wish it was on my finger still," he said. "I was very fond of it. I can't believe you've picked up on it today."

We covered many subjects, his career, his love life, his trip to the Middle East. Throughout the whole Reading the ring stayed.

It simply wouldn't go away. I could still see it on his finger.

"Do you suppose that means something?" he asked.

I heard myself say, "Your ring may have been missing for a long time. However, I believe it will be back on your finger in the near future."

And it was!

He called to tell me the story of his new carpet and the ring.

The carpet layers had to take up the old carpet to put down the new.

"I could hardly believe my ears," he said, "when one of the tradesmen asked 'Have you lost a ring?'."

And there it was! The missing ring, found at last and rescued from its hiding place under the carpet.

"I will never take it off again," he vowed. "It is on my finger for good!"

A LOST DOG

Many people consult a psychic about a missing article when, in fact, they can find it themselves with the help of their guides.

All they need to say is, "Guides, please help me find my missing item. I really need your help here."

When people phone to ask about a loss, I advise them to try this method.

Many a lost animal has been located this way, including my cattle dog, Kimbles.

Kimbles will jump a two-meter fence with hardly any effort at all. Cattle dogs have an incredible ability to spring high into the air from a standing position and are therefore hard to confine.

When I go out I have the choice of either taking her with me, or locking her in the house.

There have been times when a sudden gust of wind or thunder has startled her, and in less than a minute she has jumped our high fence and vanished.

To avoid the never-ending searching, I simply ask my guides for help.

Next, I take the first thought that comes into my head, such as "someone is returning her" or "Kimbles is at the Waggon Wheel plant nursery." This is a favorite place of hers. I suspect she likes the friendly staff.

Our guides' messages always are correct. I have never found them to be otherwise.

A man called me one night to ask if I could help with his lost dog. I knew it was with someone else and that it was all right overnight.

I also knew that it was imperative he find it very early next morning before it moved on from where it was.

When the phone rang a few days later, I was confronted by a strange dog sitting by my phone.

A dog in spirit!

Of course, I instantly knew who this spirit dog was.

He imparted his feelings to me. I became aware of how blissfully happy and contented he felt.

I was smiling at him as I answered the phone.

"My dog was killed by a car," the caller said. "Only a few moments before I found him.

"He must have tried to cross the road and was hit just before I got there. At least he was killed instantly."

The man had loved his dog and was certainly grieving over the separation.

He showed the uncommon good sense of giving a home to another dog straight away. This was intended to help the family overcome their grief. But I suspect it will unwittingly work for the grieving man as well.

THE CAT WHO WASN'T LOST

There is the delightful story of the lady who had lost her Siamese cat.

"He is not lost," I told the startled woman.

"Of course Charnea is lost. He has been gone for days. He must be terrified!"

"He's such a baby and so defenseless. Something terrible could happen to him, out there all alone."

"Charnea watches you each night as you frantically call him," I revealed.

I could "see" the end of a cul-de-sac, a vacant block of land and a cat sitting very still, under a bush.

I was aware that the cat was outwaiting its owner.

"Is it a small park? Or a vacant block that I'm looking at? I see trees and bushes towards the back of the land and I 'know' it is only a few homes away from where you live.

"To the right of the land is one small bush, the bush Charnea sits under in order to shield himself from your eyes."

"We do live a few doors from a block, leading onto a reserve along the creek. You are certainly picking that up, but you must be mistaken about Charnea hiding from me.

"He would never do that, he loves me very much."

"Of course, he loves you," I hastened to comfort her. "He adores you. He also adores another cat who happens to be in season.

"She is out every night destroying the wildlife and adding unwanted kittens to the world. Her owners don't seem to be concerned with either the environment or her safety."

I told her to take some cooked chicken down the reserve that evening and to walk slowly towards, and close to, his hiding place.

"You must act as if you know exactly where he is. Talk quietly to him as if it's perfectly normal to bring food to him at the reserve at night.

"Kneel down and place the chicken on the grass and tell Charnea to come and get his dinner."

"It is crucial that he be desexed," I found myself adding.

About a week later, I received a phone call from the now happy cat owner.

When she placed the chicken on the grass, not one, but two hungry cats came running.

Charnea's girlfriend turned out to be a friendly Abyssinian. So friendly, that she followed my cat-carrying client home and invited herself to be an overnight guest. She helped Charnea finish off the remainder of the chicken.

"You'll be pleased to know that Charnea is now desexed," my client added.

"I took the liberty of having his little friend done too. Her owners will probably never notice."

"It is the best thing for her. I told the vet she was mine."

It was the clairvoyant's turn to be shocked.

THE WIFE WITH RED HAIR

One man has a consultation with me once a year. He travels from New Zealand for Christmas, to spend a few weeks with his parents who live in Sydney.

The first year he came to me, I became "aware" of a tall woman with red hair, pointing to a wedding ring on her finger.

I asked, "Is your wife a tall woman with red hair?" and before he had time to answer, I added, "And there is another person who is identical to her.

"She's a twin, your wife is a twin!"

"But I am not married," he said. "I'm divorced. My ex-wife isn't tall and she's not a redhead.

"I'm a little anti-women at the moment, as well."

I asked my guides to only give information he could identify with. We covered many topics and he was delighted with his Reading.

At the end of the session, he mentioned the tall lady. "I can't imagine why that happened," he puzzled.

And there she was, with him again and still touching the ring on her wedding finger.

This time she was nodding as if confirming I was right the first time.

Tapping had also started on the back of my head.

Before I could stop myself, I became aware of words spilling quickly from my mouth.

"You will call me from New Zealand and tell me all about your new wife. She is a twin and she has glorious red hair.

"She is very much like a Scorpio to me and you could marry during the Leo period - that's late July into August!"

He did call from New Zealand, to confirm my prediction, and to introduce his fiancee to me over the phone.

I was thrilled to be invited to the wedding in late July, but had to decline because of commitments to lectures.

Now when he books to see me, he books for two. His beautiful Scorpio wife and himself.

A similar thing happened on another occasion.

A CHANGE OF HUSBAND

During a Reading with a client, I "picked up" on her friend from work.

"She has four children, four daughters," I said.

"Yes that's right. She does have four daughters."

"I am 'seeing' her husband. He is a caring person and has an almost outrageous personality.

"He really goes out of his way to please her. He is like a Taurus and has the bluest of eyes."

"Oh no!" she cried. "That's the man she likes. He's our boss – he owns the firm we work for.

"I will have to tell Anna you said that. She wishes he was her husband, she really likes him."

She went on to tell me that Anna's husband was a cruel and hard man, who had been reared in a country where men owned their wives and children, and controlled every part of their lives with force.

"Strange that I should 'pick up' her boss as her husband," I mused. "I'm getting confirmation on her marriage status and that's the man I see as her husband.

"I'll just go a little deeper here and try to get linear timing on that."

I went much deeper into trance and the confirmation came.

"I see her married to her boss by this time next year," I predicted.

Anna came to see me. She reminded me of her friend's Reading and said she wanted all the information I could give her.

"Don't leave anything out at all, please! Tell me the bad as well as the good. Tell me everything."

And I did!

I started with, "Say your husband's first name, repeat his first name a few times."

Immediately I tuned into the vibration of his name and, in a matter of seconds, heard myself say, "He is going to tell you he's getting a divorce, because he's tired of you.

"What he won't tell you, however, is that he is already making plans to marry a childlike girl who lives overseas.

"He has seen her lately and has also talked to her parents.

"He has made up his mind."

Anna couldn't believe her good luck.

"He has just returned from a trip back home," she said. "I know he is up to something, but I know better than to ask.

"This seems too good to be true! It would be wonderful to be free of him.

"I will probably have to give up my nice home. It doesn't matter though. I can't expect to have everything.

"I want peace of mind above anything else."

"Anna, never tell yourself that things are too good to be true," I implored. "Your subconscious mind absorbs that negative belief and your future is created out of your beliefs.

"I can see that you will get to keep your home if you play your cards right, so to speak."

"How?" she asked.

The information kept coming through. I was receiving information on how she could have an amicable divorce and be on the receiving end as well.

"I 'get' that you must appear to be upset when he tells you of his divorce plans. You must never let him suspect that you want him to go.

"You will need to become an actress!

"Believe it or not, the man does have a conscience under all that authority.

"I 'get' that you must agree with him when he tells you he is going to sell the house and leave you without anywhere to live. It is important that you look sad and agree with whatever he tells you.

"However, he will finally tell you that he will sign the house over to you.

"He will feel sorry for putting you through all the drama, and I don't see him wanting to take the children away from you. You won't have any worries over custody at all.

"His ego will tell him you have a broken heart because of him. And this is for the good.

"He will give you the house out of guilt. However, if you were to ask for it, he would refuse."

Anna came to see me frequently during the ensuing months.

The drama unfolded.

The topic of divorce had certainly surfaced.

Her husband informed her that he planned a quick divorce, with her divorcing him. His lawyer cousin handled the legal work and Anna found herself signing back-dated papers.

Instead of taking a year to end the marriage, the lawyer managed to finalize it within eight months.

At no time during this period was Anna consulted as to whether she agreed to a divorce or not, either by the lawyer or her husband.

She was informed instead that "they were getting a divorce".

During this period, their life went on as normal. The couple shared the home as if they were permanently together. A strange situation indeed.

As the settlement date grew closer, Anna affirmed all day long that the house would be hers.

Every time a negative thought crept in, she remembered to cancel it and replace it with a positive one.

She told me that her emotions were building to peak. Trying to hide the escalating excitement was not an easy task, especially over such a long period of time.

One night, the eldest of her four daughters asked her father the fateful question, "Will we still live here?"

"Yes, it is your mother's house now, I have arranged to sign it over to her tomorrow. I plan to live overseas for a few years and I leave this weekend."

Anna broke down and cried.

Within weeks, her husband had a new wife and, within months, Anna had a new husband.

A caring blue-eyed Taurus husband!

The same man I had "seen" as her husband one year previously.

"I remarried on the rebound," Anna told her shocked ex-husband and his parents.

This they could understand!

CHAPTER TEN

LEAVE BODY — WILL TRAVEL

Astral Travel during Daylight .... *Page 216*

Travel in the Light Aircraft Lane .... *Page 219*

LEAVE BODY – WILL TRAVEL

*M*any people believe an out-of-body experience to be exceptional and exciting. And of course it is.

Many of my travels are a result of programming them to happen. But travels during sleep, I find, are not always by "request".

Spontaneous travel often happens, and always it brings a sense of boundless joy.

An infinite state of bliss and incredible happiness emerge at the same time.

One floats as if by thought. There are no barriers at all, not even daylight it seems.

This I learned on a meditation weekend.

Not long after learning yet another "Type" of meditation, the teachers invited our new group to a weekend of meditation in the Blue mountains, a few hours' drive from Sydney.

I arrived with some excellent wines and an abundance of goodies to nibble on, intending to entertain a few friends with a late-night supper in my room.

We settled in on the Friday evening and enjoyed the talks, a brief meditation and supper.

We were then told that it was important to all be in bed, with lights out, by ten.

"I've never been to sleep by ten in my life," I complained to a shocked teacher - who asked me to put the wine safely in the boot of my car and to please leave it there.

Early to bed, early to rise, it seemed, was the order of the day.

ASTRAL TRAVEL DURING DAYLIGHT

I awoke at daybreak, refreshed from a good night's sleep and eager to start the day right. I sat on a chair next to my bed and meditated.

Coming out of a deeply relaxed state, I noticed that it was now fully daylight. In fact, a bright sunny morning.

I was thrilled to be spending a weekend in the town of my birth and childhood.

I stood and stretched slowly a few times and then decided to lie down on the bed for a short while.

I "awoke" to find myself floating over the gully behind the same house I lived in as a child. Just floating along effortlessly, as light as a feather.

No fear, no concern. Just delight and wonder at the miracle that was happening.

Each blade of grass was visible.

I could see every detail in the blooms of the waratahs, still growing wild in the bush surrounding the old family house.

I floated out over the Megalong Valley and back over Mount Boyce where I was born, remembering that my brother had been named Maxwell Boyce after this Mount.

I happily realized that this wasn't my first lifetime in this area.

I recognized the tracks I had taken on walkabout as a young Aborigine in another time and space.

The tracks weaved along the edge of the cliffs overlooking the valley, in and out of the sandstone rocks and coarse grasses.

My valley.

That life is just as familiar to me now, as the life I am "presently" leading.

I had "come home" twice, in the one morning, to the place of my births.

That is the first, and only, time I have astral-traveled in broad daylight.

A magical happening and the last thing I expected to spontaneously occur during a weekend of meditation.

And it is possibly one of the reasons I advise people to start with meditation, in answer to their question of "Where do I start?".

TRAVEL IN THE LIGHT AIRCRAFT LANE

When I really desire to float during my sleep, I use a technique that is often overlooked. When an answer or technique is both simple and easy, it can be passed by in place of one that takes time and effort.

I use the easy way.

I just ask!

"Guides, Higher Self, God/Goddess/All That Is, I need some help here to go astral traveling tonight. Please come with me on a wonderful adventure."

Animals also travel this way.

One night I realized that the duvet on my bed seemed to be underneath, instead of on top of me.

And not just underneath, but way down and becoming further and further away all the time.

The realization that I was floating far above the bed hit me with a huge wave of gratitude and excitement.

I floated out through the bedroom wall, down through the upstairs floor and into the family room below.

On the sofa, curled up together, were my two Siamese cats, sleeping soundly as if they were still living this life. Curled up in their favorite comfortable position at one end of the sofa.

On the thick, fluffy floor rug nearby was another feline, "Ginger", who lived almost twenty-three years in a life shared with us.

He lay stretched out full-length, as he had always done during his life.

I floated up and out through the roof, and higher and higher until the houses looked extremely small.

I looked down at the neighborhood spread out below. It looked like a road map.

"I'm floating in the light aircraft lane," I thought.

This is a lane Paul and I had flown in many times, in our little two-seater 150 Cessna aircraft, and later in a four-seater 172 Cessna.

"And now here I am, traveling without the aid of aircraft or body.

"No sign of light planes tonight though, just me alone with my silver cord, gliding to anywhere I choose.

"What would the neighbors say?" I thought.

Good point! What would the neighbors say?

My neighbors would probably wave and say "That's nice Dawn, so good to see you floating around up there."

Back over the surrounding homes I drifted, and into mine.

"This time I will float back into my body carefully, instead of jolting back into the physical world."

It's possible for souls who have left the earth-plane to enjoy the physical plane by a similar method.

Seth, the amazing energy essence personality, who channeled through Jane Roberts, apparently takes great delight in visiting an Edwardian study occasionally.

It must be fun, when one has left this lifetime, to experience a physical reality in such a way.

While the astral travelers of the earth plane are floating around, delighting in the temporary absence of a physical body, Seth would be achieving the opposite result.

I wonder if I will also have a favorite place to return to in this life after I leave?

One thing I do know, I love the life I'm living at the moment. I am enjoying this return, or as Shirley MacLaine has pointed out to us, this "Many Happy Returns".

I'm just so glad I chose this particular lifetime.

I must admit that life has improved dramatically since I formed a friendship with my entity friends Seth, Lazaris, and, of course, Roemann and Silzaar.

They all teach the joys of taking total responsibility for the reality we create.

I love being aware of what I'm creating in the future, it makes such a difference to know that I alone am responsible for the outcome of my life. I know I am in charge, and I am the one with the power over my life.

As a result I am choosing to live a totally fun-filled life. And it is much more enjoyable than having to wonder about, "What the hell is going to happen tomorrow?"

CHAPTER ELEVEN

TRANSITION

The Angel Messenger .... *Page* 227

I Won't Be at My Funeral .... *Page* 231

I, Too, Can See Angels .... *Page* 233

*People today are increasingly interested in
"out-of-body" experiences.*

*However, some of my most exciting and memorable
happenings have occurred as "in-body" experiences
- that is, while I'm still in the physical body.*

THE ANGEL MESSENGER

The night before my father's funeral I went to bed early and just sat in bed in the darkened room, reflecting on his life and wondering what it had all been about.

Dad had his dreams, like the rest of us. The sad part is, I can't remember him achieving any of them.

He had certainly missed out in the happiness stakes. His whole life centered around "doing the right thing".

At his Jehovah's Witness' funeral, he was described by his peers as a good provider, a hard worker, a friend in need and a God-fearing man.

A pillar of strength in the Jehovah's Witness' community.

And he was! My father was all that and more, as the saying goes.

No-one spoke of his dreams, or his enjoyment of life. Nobody mentioned the fun - for, in fact, there was none.

They did speak of his disappointment in his children, who did not follow in the faith.

As a child I would sit and listen to stories of his life in Queensland and his love of the land.

He would tell me that, one day, we would all go to live in the subtropical area where the states of Queensland and New South Wales meet. Aussies call this "the border area".

He never liked the Blue Mountains, just west of Sydney, where we lived. Nor the little town of Walang in the central west of New South Wales where my mother was raised and which we visited often.

His heart remained in the north-coast region.

I sat and wondered if a spiritual quest, or a life so devoid of fun, was worth it.

"I really need to see Angels," I thought. Or was this the need of the inner child?

I awoke with the strong feeling that someone else was in the room.

There was. An outline of a "person", an outline of gold light.

My cats and I sat up, alert but unafraid.

"Daddy? Dad? Is that you?"

The gold outline zigzagged a few times and then reshaped itself into wings. "Oh my goodness! An Angel. There is an Angel in my bedroom."

I knew it was communicating to me that Dad was happy, that he had found all he'd expected to find in the hereafter.

He had carried the illusion of life over with him apparently.

This is temporary and quite common. It soon wears off however, the Angel conveyed, and "knowing" takes over.

"Everyone he wanted to be there to meet him, was there, including an aspect of you yourself, Dawn."

"My father had a Jehovah's Witness' greeting? On the other side? And I was there to meet him? An aspect of me was there greeting him? And I didn't know about it?"

I must be dreaming and yet, I "knew" without any doubt that this was no dream.

"I wonder why he didn't come himself?" I thought.

"You are wondering why he didn't come himself," the Angel conveyed.

"He thought it would be more fun to have an Angel call on you, Dawn.

"He has never admitted it before, but he has always known that you can see Angels!"

"Oh, my God. My father is finally having fun. My father is having fun!"

I laughed until I couldn't laugh any longer. Tears of joy ran down my cheeks and for hours I couldn't take the smile off my face.

I didn't go back to bed that night at all. I was on a high and it was one of the happiest nights of my life, spent in the kitchen drinking endless cups of tea and reliving Dad's message again and again.

I WON'T BE AT MY FUNERAL

On the morning of my uncle's funeral, I talked to a few friends on my channel board, including my board guide, John.

John spelled out the words, "Do you want to speak to Ray?"

"Ray? Uncle Ray? Yes I'd love to talk to him. Thank you John."

Instantly he was through.

"Is that you Uncle Ray? I'm going to your funeral today."

"Don't bother Dawn, I'm not going. It will be two boring services with the same boring minister."

"Two services? Are you sure? Why would you have two services?"

"I'm not having them, I won't be there. You will have to sit through two boring services if you go."

"Uncle Ray, I must go - to pay my respects, as they say."

"Waste of time Dawn, believe me! May wants to talk to you."

May came through to have our usual morning chat. May was my mother in this life and Uncle Ray's sister.

I did go to his funeral.

After the lengthy church service we were instructed to follow the hearse to the crematorium, where we were ushered inside and shown where to sit.

Out from behind the crematorium curtain, came the same minister. The very same minister who gave the service at the church.

I listened in amazement as he delivered the very same sermon all over again, to the same group of people.

"Uncle Ray, you were right. You were absolutely right." I repeated silently, over and over. "You were spot on!"

It was hard not to smile at my brother's funeral, too. He made it almost impossible for me to look sad.

I, TOO, CAN SEE ANGELS

I had almost completed a Reading for a regular client. He makes the six-hour trip every six months from a cattle station in the north-west of the state.

He calls to confirm his appointment about a week prior. "It's your favorite 'cow-cocky' here

Dawn, just confirming that I will be seeing you next week."

On one occasion I said to him, "I get the name Max around you, and the two of you have been meaning to get together. I think you have left it too late."

I said the "you have left it too late" part, before I realized I'd said it.

I was shocked at myself for having allowed that message to come straight through. I'm usually much more careful about conveying such messages.

"Max is an old friend, my mate," said my cow-cocky.

"And I see all these trucks around you both."

"We drove trucks together for years."

Suddenly my brother's face appeared next to this man. The face of my brother Max.

"I hope his name's not Max Pemberton," I cried.

"No, it's not. But please tell me all, you must tell me all."

"There is a stroke, a heart attack and sadness there. I am so sorry, but you wanted to know."

Then I added, "It is a dual message for both of us today. I saw my brother's face next to yours."

The portable phone rang. I walked to my desk and hesitated before picking it up.

My nephew was on the line. My brother Max's son!

"Dad has had a stroke and a heart attack. He has been taken to hospital."

Since that day, I no longer answer the phone during consultations. The answering machine stays on.

For three days, the family gathered at Max's bedside, talking to his unconscious body, asking him to wake up and telling him to hang onto life.

On the third day, as the Sister gently turned him over, a wave of indescribable joy rushed from him to me.

It swept into my entire body, right down to the bones and even as it left me, it stayed with me.

I stood transfixed as I actually "felt" and "saw" it take off. The wave came from Max to me and then up through the ceiling and was gone.

The whole family was falling apart, and here was I with a tingling body and a feeling of exhilaration.

I tried to do the "decent" thing. I tried to conform and look sad, when I really wanted the world to know the joy he was experiencing.

I know he shared his experience with *me* simply because he knew he could.

A few hours after Max's death, my husband rang from Sydney.

"I've been talking to Max," he exclaimed.

"Talking to Max?"

"Yes, talking to Max! I picked him up on the channel board. I had this strong desire to try to get him on the board and he came straight through.

"We've been conversing for over an hour and he is so excited about going."

I looked around the room guiltily, to see if the family were listening to my conversation. They would never understand.

They were absorbed in conversation together and would not be able to hear.

"Tell me what he had to say," I said. "Tell me!"

"He said he really wanted to go, he had done everything he wanted to do in this life and he was bored. He wanted to move on.

"He also said that the reason he'd finished everything off around the home was so he could be free to go. He said, too, that you and Roy would leave his funeral early and travel northwest."

"That doesn't make any sense at the moment. I wonder why we would travel north instead of south," I puzzled.

"We can't leave our own brother's funeral early. There would have to be an emergency of some type for that to happen."

Roy had been unable to contact his son Keith, whose spiritual name is Pan, and the funeral was drawing close.

Pan had been notified of his Uncle Max's passing, but no acknowledgment had been received from him.

A child had phoned in a few times trying to leave a message with Max's family about snakebite.

Assuming that the young person was phoning the wrong number, the grieving wife and children didn't take any notice.

When Roy and I heard of the phone calls, we realized that the caller could be Pan's son.

And, of course, it was! Pan had been bitten not once, but three times, on his hands by a tiger snake.

He had tried to pull the snake's head away from where it had its fangs buried in his hand. As soon as the snake let go of one hand, it found that it was free to swing around and bury the old fangs in the other hand.

"A sort of musical snakebite," as Pan later described the event.

Max was right. Roy and I did leave as early as we politely could and traveled for a few hundred kilometers, north-west to Lismore hospital.

On arrival we found a very ill young man, refusing to have an antidote administered.

The doctors were not happy with him at all. Pan told me later, after he eventually recovered, that at the time he could actually feel himself "slipping away".

This was one day I would never forget.

Max's body was buried on a hillside and, unlike our parents, he did attend his own funeral. He was there, commenting on the view and leaning against his coffin.

"Thank goodness for dark sunglasses," I thought as he deliberately tried to make me laugh.

"Don't do that. Please don't try to make me laugh," I silently implored him. "Stop it, and stop leaning all over your coffin."

"Well, it's my coffin," he teased, "It is mine, isn't it?

"Oh! and guess what, Sis, guess what! You're not the only one to see Angels."

"I can see Angels!"

It was then I started to cry.

CHAPTER TWELVE

I Can See Angels

FROM THE DIARY OF A TEN YEAR OLD

Dear Dawn,

Who am I? Why am I here?

Why am I here in this school, with this group of children?

Is life really true, or is life made up of dreams?

Is it a dream that we have a nice teacher named Miss Avis, or is she real?

I know that I have lived before. Why is it that I know?

Why is it that I don't know anyone else who knows? Why is it that everyone thinks it's not nice to talk about living before?

Is the world a big dream, or is the world a lot of dreams?

Who am I really?

I know that I am a person who loves animals.

Cats are my favorite animals. When I grow up I will have lots of cats.

I love cats, tap dancing, ballet, composition, English, sewing and spelling best of all. I like spinach and peanut butter, too.

I like everyone at school. I like myself, too, but I won't tell anybody that, because it is wrong to like yourself.

Why is it wrong to like yourself? Who said it is wrong to like yourself?

Why is it wrong to see Angels?

I can see Angels!

The only time Miss Avis punished me, was when I handed in my diary. She had asked if she could read it.

Her words rang in my ears for the remainder of the day.

She said she had no idea what she should say to me about the diary. She just knew that she should administer some sort of punishment.

"This is a very sad day for me," she said as she handed my diary back.

I sat in shame, and alone, outside on the school porch for the remainder of the lesson.

I put my now infamous diary away. I never took it to school again.

That night, as I lay in bed, I wondered why I had taken it to school in the first place. I also wondered why it had shocked Miss Avis so much.

I was feeling sad and depressed and I had the overwhelming desire to float right up over the world and watch down from above.

"I could just visit my Angels for a little while and come straight back."

This thought gave me a warm comforting glow as I drifted off to sleep.

I "woke" to find myself floating high up above my bed.

The bedroom was in darkness and yet I could see every item in the room. Not in color though, it was more like black and white; a subtle, soft black and white.

I felt blissfully happy and light and exhilarated and free, all at the same time.

The silver cord that trailed from my floating self, way down to my body, didn't constrain my freedom in any way.

I liked my silver cord.

I looked down at my sleeping body, with the head on the pillow and the long plait of hair trailing across the bed, and smiled at my stuffed koala safely cradled on one arm.

My favorite toy!

I drifted further up, over the tops of my father's turkey sheds, and saw five-thousand restless turkeys, trying to sleep through the hot night.

Rover, our faithful Kelpie dog, sat in the yard looking up in my direction.

My journey didn't appear to concern him at all. "Rover knows I'm safe," I thought.

Higher and higher I rose, far up above the farm and in amongst the clouds.

I felt so at peace, as if the fiasco at school had never happened. It was no longer important.

I had come to make contact with my Angels.

And I did!

They appeared as they had done so many years before. Small balls of light, far off in the distance, moving slowly towards me, bringing love and peace.

"Where are their wings?" I asked of the Universe.

And there they were. Golden wings on golden balls of light, coming to give comfort again to this child.

"I can see them," I smiled.

"I can see Angels!"

APPENDIX

The following books and inspirational materials are highly recommended by Dawn Rawlings...
– Listed in alphabetical order

Absolute Happiness ..... Michael Domeyko Rowland
A Return to Love .... Marianne Williamson
Creative Visualization .... Shakti Gawain
Don't Worry Be Hopi .... Jo Buchanan
Going Within .... Shirley MacLaine
Jonathan Livingstone Seagull .... Richard Bach
Lazaris Interview Books 1 & 2 .... Lazaris
Love Yourself, Heal Your Life .... Louise L. Hay
Miracles .... Stuart Wilde
Quantum Healing .... Deepak Chopra, M.D.
Seth Speaks .... Jane Roberts
The Celestine Prophecy .... James Redfield
The Color Compass .... Tricia Skerry
The Crystal Cards .... Dawn Rawlings
The Dreamers Guide to the Galaxy ..... Leon Nacson
You Can Heal Your Life .... Louise L. Hay

MEET THE AUTHOR

After reading this book you may want to hear Dawn Rawlings in person. Dawn regularly conducts seminars and workshops in almost every English-speaking country in the world, as well as a number of non-English speaking countries, working through a translator.

FOR INFORMATION ABOUT HER SEMINARS WRITE TO:
DownUnder Productions Pty Ltd
95E Seven Hills Rd
Baulkham Hills NSW 2153
AUSTRALIA
Phone: **(02) 838 8783**
Fax: **(02) 838 8750**

International callers
Phone: **61 2 838 8783** or
Fax: **61 2 838 8750**